The Strength to Shift

REVEAL • HEAL • TRANSFORM

THE
STRENGTH
TO SHIFT

10 Inspiring Tales
of Change and Transformation

KELLY SNIDER

Founder • **EPIC** EXCHANGES

EPIC EXCHANGES MEDIA

Published by Epic Exchanges Media, September 2024
ISBN: 9781777555245

Editor: Danielle Anderson
Proofreader: Deborah Sauro
Front Cover Illustration: *Changing Tides* by Missy Caswell
Cover Design and Typesetting: Tara Eymundson

DISCLAIMER: Readers of this publication agree that neither Kelly Snider nor her publisher will be held responsible or liable for damages that may be alleged as resulting directly or indirectly from the use of this publication. Neither the publisher nor the author can be held accountable for the information provided by, or actions resulting from, accessing these resources. This book is not intended in any way to replace professional healthcare or mental health advice, but to support it.

Dedication

*To everyone who is right now living a story
that is worth sharing—your story matters too.*

Testimonials

"It's definitely through our stories that we learn about ourselves and others...it's through our stories that we raise our level of consciousness for all human beings. It is through our stories that our heart breaks for others and shines a light of compassion that stays with us not only for ourselves, for the storytellers, but for humanity – those we meet in grocery stores, in the checkout line, seemingly taking a long time to get through, and those behind the deli counter... all the places where we encounter the faceless people in our midst...it's the stories of people that make us look into each other's eyes and know them."
Shahin Najak, M.Ed
Mindfulness Coach, Toronto, ON

* * *

"Kelly has a GIFT. Her incredible ability to draw a person's story out of them in such a beautiful and loving way – for the reader to relate to, be inspired by, and to heal through. Kelly is facilitating healing, amplifying women's voices through another magnificent collection of female truths."
Emily Scott
Artist, Tucson, AZ

Contents

Acknowledgements

I'm so thrilled to be finally able to follow up our first anthology, *The Gift in Your Story*, with this collection of stories from another group of inspiring women.

It's not easy to be open, honest, and vulnerable about our journeys and then publish them for all the world to read. On behalf of each one of these authors, we want to thank our families, friends, and other supporters for their overwhelming encouragement and support.

To my amazing co-authors in this book, thank you for trusting me through this process, and for revisiting and sharing some of the most transformational times in your lives; the times that have often included intense difficulty and pain, but that have resulted in who you are today and brought out even more of the best of you. Thank you for being willing to share your journey in the hopes that it might help someone else.

And to you, our readers: I hope that you see some of your own journey within these pages, and that you find a desire to dive into your own stories, discover your own strength, and pass that on to someone else.

Introduction

By Kelly Snider

Eighteen years ago, I first realized that even a small part of my story—of making an intentional change to improve my life—was inspirational to strangers. Before that, I had shied away from sharing my story, worried that it might paint me as a victim or that people might pity me. That was the last thing I wanted. I wanted to be seen as strong and capable. But when someone told me how much my decision to take time to care for myself had inspired them, I realized my perception had been wrong. If my story could help just one person, then I *had* to share it.

That moment began a long journey that brought me not only to discovering how to share my own experiences, but also to helping others find their own voices and speak up about all they learned in the process of living with and through their life challenges.

Sometimes these challenges are overwhelming events that shake us to the core and redefine our entire lives. One moment we are cruising along, comfortable in our routines and familiar surroundings; the next, we are thrown into the unknown, facing challenges and obstacles that test our faith, make us face some hard truths, and even push us to the brink. But it is in these moments of upheaval, of uncertainty, of even doubt in ourselves and our abilities that our true strength rises to the surface to help us bring about change for the better.

Other times, these challenges are more subtle. They lurk at the edges of our lives, providing a constant reminder that something is not quite as it should be. Then that moment of realization hits, shining light into that darkness, and we experience a transformation that shapes our perspectives and priorities.

At its core, *The Strength to Shift* is a celebration of resilience, courage, and the unquenchable human spirit. It is a reminder that no matter what life throws our way, we have the power to rise above, to transform, and to emerge stronger and more resilient than ever before. These moments, these *shifts*, define who we are and who we become. Within these pages is a collection of narratives from ten women who have faced these adversities and emerged stronger, wiser, and more empowered. Each author has faced their own unique set of challenges, yet their experience resonates with a shared truth: we all have the capacity to adapt, evolve, and even thrive.

This book is more than just a collection of individuals recounting their experiences; it is a testament to the power of storytelling. By sharing their truths with vulnerability and authenticity, these women invite each one of us to reflect on our own lives, to embrace our vulnerabilities, and to find inspiration and transformation in the shared human experience.

As you embark on this journey through the lives of these authors, may their stories serve as a reminder that no matter how daunting the challenges may seem, we all possess the inner strength to shift, grow, and embrace the fullness of our potential. For in the end, it is not our circumstances that define us, but our courage to confront them and emerge transformed.

1

There's Gotta Be Something More

By Kelly Snider

*"There is no passion to be found
playing small—in settling for a life that is less
than the one you are capable of living."*

— Nelson Mandela

There's Gotta Be Something More

By Kelly Snider

As a child, I went through several different visions of my perfect future self. At first I wanted to do nothing but ride horses, but that changed around the age of nine or ten when I alternately wanted to be a secretary, a nurse, or a teacher. I was an avid reader, and from what I was reading in my books at the time, it seemed like these were the optimal choices for a woman.

My first paying job actually came at around that same age, when I spent my spring break filing invoices at my grandfather's company. He had started a dental supply business that also employed my grandmother, mother, and uncle. It wasn't exciting work, but it was a taste of office life. I felt grown up going to the office every day with my mom and having a specific responsibility, and I definitely liked the paycheque at the end of the week.

And of course, as with many adolescents, I did a lot of babysitting throughout my high school years. This usually entailed playing with the kids until their bedtime, getting them to bed, and then watching television until their parents came home. Again, not exciting, but I was earning money.

However, none of this really felt like a "real job"—one that I found on my own rather than through family or friends or family friends—where I could make some real money. So, when I was seventeen, I wandered the mall with my resume and asked any place that looked interesting if they were hiring. A couple weeks later, I landed my first retail job at a small toy store.

The job wasn't as glamourous as I had thought it might be. For the first three months, all I did was dust and clean shelves. Box after box of LEGO, Barbies, and Hot Wheels needed wiping. Every four-hour shift was filled with endless cleaning. However, as the Christmas season got closer and our store got busier, I started to be given more responsibility. It still wasn't exciting, but at least the time passed more quickly.

Once the store got truly busy, though, I really enjoyed the work. I loved interacting with customers and helping them find the perfect gift for the children in their lives.

This was the beginning of a series of jobs in the retail world over the next several years, working my way through a few different companies and roles: an assistant buyer for an office supply company, an assistant manager for a chocolatier, and a manager of a men's clothing boutique. Each job had its perks, but none felt like a lasting career. I was always looking for ways to learn something new, challenge myself, and expand my knowledge, and in retail the work could quickly become repetitive. It wouldn't take long for me to get bored and feel like I'd reached the limit of my potential within the company, and then I would be off looking for a new challenge to take on.

I was working with a growing aromatherapy company when I discovered an opportunity to move out of the retail store and into a position in their office. This felt like a wonderful new challenge for me; since the office was located in their warehouse space, where they blended the oils and created all their products, I would get to learn more about the business side of the company. They were growing quickly and needed some systems put in place to support their expanding customer base and move it beyond the local market. One of my goals was to start a mail-order business to support their retail locations—this was before shopping online was a thing.

I was really excited for this new challenge. Because the company was growing so quickly, I felt like there would be less repetition and more potential for my own growth and development. However, after spending about eighteen months in this position and having a limited ability to take on more responsibility, I decided it was time to move on once again. This time, an opportunity came up to try something completely different: I was asked to spend time with my new nephew as his nanny.

This became the first of three different nanny positions in which I helped the families through specific challenges for short periods of time, such as the summer season when school was out. Meanwhile, I was still trying to figure out exactly what I wanted to do for a career. I wasn't going to be a nanny forever, that was for sure; I loved the children, but this world of arts and crafts and mealtime and naptime and reading the same children's books over and over still felt too limited and small. This wasn't *it* for me.

Throughout this time, I had been continuing my schooling. I had completed my university degree, a bachelor of arts in psychology, as well as a business management diploma program, a certification course for travel agents, and a ten-month diploma in digital and recording arts to learn sound engineering. I was following my interests and exploring potential career paths, but each time I hit a stumbling block when it came to finding meaningful employment.

My BA in psychology was a four-year degree that I knew wouldn't immediately lead to a career. Truly working in the field would require more study and a master's program, and by the time I graduated I really didn't want to do any more classes, papers, and exams. The business management program felt the same. It was a great start, and I learned many things that I was able put to work in some of my jobs, but I felt like I needed more — more courses, more schooling — to truly create a meaningful career.

I applied to travel agencies after completing my certification course, and even offered to work for free in some kind of volunteer internship position to prove myself, but even those attempts were met with strong denials. The travel industry was in the midst of some huge changes at the time due to the rise of all-inclusive resorts and internet bookings, so there were fewer jobs available throughout the entire industry.

With sound engineering, I pursued that diploma because I loved music and theatre. I had done some volunteering with a community theatre program, working behind the scenes as a stage manager and in the sound booth, and the idea of working live shows and being on the road really appealed to me. However, the industry was still very male-dominated, and the entry-level positions were as roadies for touring productions. There wasn't a lot of room for women in these roles for a variety of reasons, but mostly because of the physical requirements, including heavy lifting—not to mention the lodging arrangements needed to accommodate a single female among an all-male crew.

When my final nanny position ended with the beginning of a new school year, I wasn't sure which way to turn. I was feeling discouraged and, quite honestly, like a failure. I had all this education, yet I still wasn't climbing the corporate ladder or doing any of the things I thought were synonymous with success. I wanted to find a fulfilling, exciting career, yet I still had bills to pay. So, I went back to what I knew. With all my experience in retail, those jobs were the easy path to receiving a paycheque, and I quickly found a position in a department store. It wasn't going to be my dream job, but at least it would provide an income.

The day arrived for my first four-hour shift at the store, and I spent that time alone in one of the back storerooms, opening boxes and hanging up fall and winter clothing. This was not even close to what I enjoyed about working retail: helping customers find exactly what they were looking for. By the end of the first hour, my back was hurting from maneuvering boxes filled with heavy winter coats. At the end of the second hour, I was questioning whether this was worth the money. By the end of the third hour, my emotions were getting the better of me. I was frustrated and upset and questioning why I was here in the first place. I wasn't making phenomenal money, and I didn't love the work. In fact, I was hating every moment and counting the seconds until I could leave. And it was just the first day!

This couldn't be all there was to being an adult—working a job I hated just to take home a meager paycheque every two weeks. And then, a thought hit me. I didn't take this job because it was something I loved to do; I took it out of desperation. And that thought felt worse than the infinite opening of boxes and hanging of clothes.

In that moment, I decided nothing was worth this misery in which I found myself. This wasn't in any way my dream, or even something I would enjoy doing on a regular basis. I could feel my spirit withering away, and I decided that I would never again take a job just for the money. I needed more. I needed to feel like I was contributing in some way, that I was making a difference. I needed more than just punching a time clock. I needed purpose.

As the final moments of my four-hour shift ticked away, I found a new resolve. I finished my task, left the storeroom as organized as possible, and went to find my manager. I told her that my shift was over, explained how I'd left things for the next employee, and told her I was leaving—and that I wouldn't be back. This job wasn't the right fit for me.

I felt intense relief walking out the door, like a massive black cloud had blown away. But at the same time, I wondered, "Now what?" I still needed a job, an income, a career path. I now knew that I didn't want to just take *any* job, and that I needed challenge, growth, and purpose. But what did that look like? And what options were actually available to me?

Then, a memory popped up. I remembered hearing or reading that if you wanted to find your path, think about what you love doing so much that you would do it for free. And as I thought about that, I realized I was already volunteering my time doing something that combined all my interests and provided me with challenge, growth, and purpose.

A couple of years beforehand, one of my friends was planning to go on a mission trip with a well-known international organization called Youth With A Mission. In order to participate, she had to raise the money to pay her way on this several-months-long trip to Vanuatu, a group of islands in the South Pacific Ocean. She had a lot of family and friends who wanted to help and encourage her, but not all of them could give money toward her goal. However, she is a creative person and dabbled in different kinds of art, so I helped her organize an afternoon tea featuring an auction of donated art pieces from all those friends and family members. There were quilts, paintings, photographs, sketches, and even some baked goods. And all these people, plus more from her workplace and church, came to support and celebrate her that afternoon. In a couple of hours, we raised over $2,000 for her trip.

For this tea, we borrowed a large gathering space from a local group that supported the homeless. When they arrived to lock up after our event, they were blown away by the fact that we could raise that much money in one afternoon. So, they asked me if I would help them do something similar for their community open house a couple of months later. They had a room full of donated items including art, brand new small appliances, furniture, kid's toys, and other miscellaneous items they didn't know what to do with. It took a lot of sorting and organizing, but in the end we were able to auction off most of these treasures during that open house, which attracted people from all across the city. The organization was truly grateful for the almost $6,000 raised for their mission of providing a helping hand to those down on their luck.

These two experiments (and successes) led to other events, and I loved planning every one of them. I got to put so many of my interests and skills into play: organization, strategic planning and budgeting, décor, and design. I was even able to bring in lighting and sound elements. At the same time, I was helping friends and organizations do good work in the world. I felt like my small contributions had a reach beyond my community.

Now that I had identified something I loved enough that I would do it for free, and was in fact already doing for free, how could I turn it into a career path? Was that even possible? I didn't know anyone who had made a career out of planning events unless they were on an enormous scale, like concert tours or opening nights for theatre companies. Maybe that would be a place to start? So, I started looking for someone to hire me. This was the later-nineties, so I started scouring want ads in newspapers and job boards, looking for any possible opportunity. I searched for events, concerts, fundraising, and more. Within a week, there it was: a national charity was looking for an event co-ordinator for their annual gala.

I applied.

I had no idea if I was even qualified as I had no professional references to give them. But what I did have were skills I had developed through my seemingly random experience, both in my school courses and in all my jobs and volunteering for friends. I had business acumen, the ability to work with all kinds of people, knowledge of the technicalities around good sound set-ups, and some incredible organizational skills, problem-solving skills, and more.

I was thrilled when I was called for an interview within a couple of days. I was then hired on the spot and given a year-long contract to work solely on their black-tie gala and auction for 600 guests.

That first paid event gig was a little trial-by-fire. I was working with committees who had been with this event and organization a lot longer than I, and many of them had very strong personalities. It was often a balancing act to manage their hopes and expectations with the needs of the charity, while also making them feel heard and appreciated. However, they helped me learn about the event and the charity from a different angle through sharing their own experiences. I also had the responsibility of managing the invitation design, printing, and mailing; collecting and categorizing auction items; designing the sponsorship program; monitoring ticket sales; determining table seating; and more. It was overwhelming, but it was also exhilarating and exciting.

Then the day finally came, and we welcomed the guests to our "Sunset at the Taj Mahal" themed evening. After seeing everyone be amazed by the event, all the hours and days spent planning, organizing, and executing every minute detail was worth it. The night was a resounding success; we more than doubled the funds raised the previous year.

That experience was the beginning of more than twenty-five years of event production. While my niche and expertise quickly homed in on the fundraising gala dinner and auction, I also had the opportunity to work on benefit concerts, golf tournaments, conferences, and home and design tours. I even organized a ten-week road trip for a group of motorcyclists, spanning all the continental United States and the Canadian provinces. I've met and worked with Grammy-award winning musicians, acclaimed actors, Olympic medallists, and more. And through these events I have played a part in raising over fifteen million dollars net for charities around the world.

Event management provided me with all the things I had been looking for in a career. One was challenge, which came from always taking on new events. I determined that if I had the opportunity, I wanted to do an event at least twice: once so I could learn the event and the organization behind it, and the second time so I could have an opportunity to make changes and refinements that would take it to another level. I also wanted a career that helped me grow, and each event I ran had an impact on both my work and my personal life. I learned so much about myself and my style of interacting with various personalities; I was also frequently given additional opportunities to learn new skills within each organization. Finally, I wanted a career that gave me purpose, which came from there being something bigger at play with every event. I helped raise funds for much-needed research, equipment, services, education, and other programs to benefit people in need, whether in my city or on the other side of the world. As a bonus, I had many opportunities to travel, meet people from all kinds of backgrounds, and learn from many experts.

This road was never easy. There were obstacles, arguments, and lessons all along the way. More than once, I was pushed to my limit emotionally, psychologically, and physically. But with every challenge I faced, I discovered something I wanted to do differently or better, some way I wanted to grow and change, as well as a new plan for how I wanted to show up in the world.

When I think back to that day in the department store backroom, I see it as the day my path—my life—changed. When I decided that I could never again take a job (or make a decision) out of desperation for money, I was forced to take a step back and really think about what I wanted. I still remind myself of that moment today whenever the urge to take the easy way out tempts me, because I know that my values of challenge, growth, and purpose have so much more importance to my mental health and well-being.

About Kelly Snider

Kelly Snider is an acclaimed event producer who excels in highlighting her clients' stories, needs, and goals. Her more than twenty-five years of story-focused events have raised over fifteen million dollars for charities around the world to date and she continues to consult with organizations and their events to maximize their impact and the guest experience.

Since the advent of the pandemic a few years ago, Kelly has shifted her focus to supporting and inspiring others through sharing the stories that connect us all. She is the author and publisher of two best-selling books, *Your Story Your Strength* and *The Gift in Your Story*—her first collaborative effort that achieved eleven number one rankings on Amazon. Her generosity in sharing her personal stories of overcoming adversity and challenge has emboldened thousands to find the freedom and strength to share their own.

Through The Power of Story Conference, her Epic Exchanges podcast, and her books, Kelly helps people find the true gifts within their stories and then share them in order to inspire and transform others.

www.kellysniderauthor.com

2

Surviving the Storm

By Kelly Mariah

"When we are no longer able to change a situation, we are challenged to change ourselves."

— Viktor Frankl

Surviving the Storm

By Kelly Mariah

September 7, 2011, was a typical dark and dreary fall day in Ohio. There was a drizzle of rain off and on throughout the day that was more of a nuisance than anything. That morning, I got my youngest, who was in first grade at the time, off to school, came home, ate my breakfast, and drank my morning cup of coffee. My oldest, Tommy, who was turning twenty-one soon, had the day off work, so we decided to sit in the family room together and watch *Cold Case Files*. We both enjoyed discussing the facts of the cases and seeing them get solved, knowing that the criminals responsible were finally put behind bars.

Over the summer, Tommy had decided that he wanted to become a police officer. He had the skills for it, and I believed he would make an amazing police officer one day. Even so, I was a bit scared of the risks involved. I remember the loving way he attempted to reassure me and calm my nerves by telling me he wasn't afraid to die; while I appreciated his effort, it was difficult to hear him say those words. I immediately felt anxious. However, I pushed my feelings aside to show support. He had been struggling to figure out what he wanted to do with his life, like so many young adults do at that age. He had tried college but came home after his first year confused and feeling like a failure. We had reassured him that it was okay, and that he would figure it out. Now that he had, I didn't want to do anything to discourage him.

Later that afternoon, Tommy picked up his little sister from school and took her home so that I could meet two friends for our weekly book group. The book we were studying, *What Did You Expect?* by Paul David Tripp, was intended to encourage a deeper relationship with your marriage partner. One of the ways it did this was by posing some difficult questions for the reader to consider, and my friends and I had been working through them together.

At the same time, I had also been reading through the Book of Job in the Bible. Job's persistent faith even after experiencing the tragic and devastating loss of his children, his possessions, and his health intrigued me. The questions from our book study coupled with my curiosity about Job's faith led to some very thought-provoking and soul-searching questions. Little did I know the question that had given me the most difficulty would turn out to be key to surviving the unthinkable that was lurking at my doorstep, waiting to devour me.

In our study, my friends and I considered how we would respond if the worst thing we could imagine, whatever that might be, actually happened in our marriage. Would it be a deal breaker, or would we still be committed to the relationship? We went one step further and asked ourselves how our walk with faith might change in light of the worst thing imaginable taking place. Would it be a deal breaker in our relationship with God, or would we choose to continue to follow Him anyway?

I had multiple answers depending on which "worst thing" might happen. If my husband had an affair, I wasn't sure I could commit to staying in the relationship, but I knew I was committed to continuing my faith journey.

I delved even deeper into my heart to consider if there was *any* circumstance that could cause me to walk away from my faith. This question deeply challenged me, and I wrestled with it greatly. While an affair wouldn't cause me to turn away from my faith, I struggled to say the same thing in the event my husband died. Could I live without him? That question haunted me; it was probably my biggest fear. In the end, I decided that if that happened, I would still choose to follow God anyway.

My two friends and I had great discussions that afternoon, and I left feeling hopeful and empowered. When I got home around 6:30 p.m., my husband and youngest daughter were preparing to go on a quick trip to the grocery store, something they did together often. I did not enjoy grocery shopping at all and rarely went along, but when they asked if I wanted to join them, for some reason I was persuaded to say yes. It was a Wednesday night, so my older daughter was at marching band practice. Tommy was sitting in his recliner in the basement, watching TV and trying to register for classes at our local community college to pursue becoming a police officer. The classes were to begin the following day, so he was under some last-minute pressure to get everything sorted out. I remember opening the basement door and calling down to let him know I was going to the store with his father and his sister. I told him we wouldn't be gone long and asked if he could let our dog, Daisy, outside in a little bit. He said he would take care of Daisy, and we said our love-yous and see-you-laters.

The three of us went to the store, which was about fifteen minutes away. It was unusually crowded that night, and getting through the aisles was like being stuck in rush-hour traffic. We were going nowhere fast. The trip was taking much longer than expected, causing my husband to be irritated and extremely frustrated.

A few minutes after 8:00 p.m., when we were about to make our way to the checkout, Tommy called my husband. I could hear the upset tone of Tommy's voice. Online registration had closed at eight, and Tommy had missed the deadline, so he was unable to sign up for the fall semester. He was feeling like he failed again. This only added to my husband's frustration, and in a gruff tone he abruptly cut off the conversation. Before hanging up, he told Tommy we were about to check out, we would be home soon, and we would talk about it then. I realized that Tommy didn't know that he could still register by going in-person to the registrar and paying a late fee. I told my husband I'd drive down to the college with Tommy the next morning and help him sort it out.

The lines at the checkout were backed up four and five deep, so it took us much longer than expected to get to the front, pay, load our groceries into the car, and get home. When we pulled into the driveway, the misty rain was turning into a downpour. As we quickly unloaded the groceries, my older daughter arrived home early from band practice, which had been cancelled due to the weather. She helped us finish unloading.

Once we got the groceries into the house, I opened the basement door to yell down and let Tommy know we were home. As soon as I opened the door, I could see that something was terribly wrong. I bolted down the stairs as fast as I could, screaming out his name and yelling upstairs for someone to call 911.

Everything seemed to be in slow motion. I was unusually calm and went into rescue mode. Incredibly, I was able to think very clearly in that moment. It had been about five years since I last had CPR training, but I began doing breaths and compressions. I kept waiting for him to gasp, begin breathing, and wake up just like you see in the movies, but that didn't happen. I knew it was not working. Oh God! Not this, anything but this! PLEASE, NO, LORD, NOT THIS!

Desperation crashed over me as I became physically exhausted, and my emotions began to overtake me. I was briefly overjoyed and relieved to hear the police arrive, but it seemed like they were moving so slowly— like they weren't doing anything. I wanted to scream at them to hurry up and save my son.

The police officers soon encouraged me to leave Tommy's side. I hesitantly and tearfully complied. Anxiety squeezed my chest as they gently helped me upstairs, knowing there was nothing else I could do. I stumbled into the dark living room and dropped to my knees in the middle of the floor, choking out deep sobs and wails. Complete blackness enveloped my entire being. I don't know how long I laid there, but the next thing I remember was becoming aware that someone was holding me. It was my dear friend who I had been with at the book study earlier that afternoon. My husband had called her. He had been hard to understand, but he told her that Tommy had taken his life and kept saying, "please come." She hadn't been sure what she was walking into, but she knew it was not good.

Everything was so surreal, like I was in some sort of time warp. My body was numb, and my face and lips felt tingly from near hyperventilation. My mind was racing from one thing to another. Why was it taking the police so long to come and tell me that they had saved him? I just wanted to wake up from this hellish nightmare. It had to be a nightmare, right? This could not be real. Why is this happening? This can't be happening!

Once reality began to set in, my husband and I realized that we had to find a way to reach our second-born son, who was at college in Alabama nine and a half hours away. He had just begun his freshman year, and we had moved him into his dorm only two weeks earlier. We needed to reach him quickly because information was beginning to get out on social media, some of which was incorrect. We had to deliver the unfathomable, horrific news that his brother had taken his life over the phone, which was one of the most difficult things we had to do in the aftermath of this tragedy. Family and friends made arrangements for him to fly home the next morning, taking care not only of the logistics but also the cost of the flight as well. My sister-in-law even flew down to meet him so that he would not have to travel back home alone.

Late that night, after everyone had gone and we were left to ourselves, my husband, our girls, and I and all climbed into our king-sized bed and literally clung to one another all night long. As we lay there, my swollen eyes stung with tears, my throat was dry and raw from heaving cries, and my entire body would involuntarily jerk every few minutes. Neither me nor my husband slept that night, or for many nights thereafter. The next several months were a complete blur.

As I write this, it has been nearly thirteen years since we lost Tommy, though in some respects it still feels like it happened yesterday. Through my journey of grief and healing, I have discovered several things. One is that you never "get over" losing someone you love. The sharpness of the pain begins to ease as time goes by and healing takes place, but it never goes away, nor should we expect it to. The deep wound of losing someone you love leaves a nasty scar.

Something else I learned is that everyone grieves differently. We are all unique individuals with different physical, mental, and emotional needs as we process our pain. For me, it was very difficult to concentrate for any length of time; I had great difficulty reading and struggled to retain anything I had just read. This made it very hard to continue to pursue my career in financial services and serve my clients to the best of my ability. For my husband, on the other hand, getting back to the classroom and teaching his students seemed to help his frame of mind greatly. There isn't a right or wrong way to grieve, so the best gift we can give to someone who is grieving is to allow them the space to do it in their own way, without judgement.

And finally, I learned how to move through this challenging time and find a way to get back to some semblance of a normal life. Because of this, I often get asked to share a few of the things that helped me in my healing journey. There are four "tools" that I believe helped the most.

My support system is one such tool. Our family, friends, and community were an amazing support; we wouldn't have made it through without them. They brought us round the clock meals for many weeks. They sent us gifts of all kinds, including gift cards for meals, entertainment, and sometimes envelopes of money for whatever we might need. They put activity baskets together for my youngest daughter. They knit prayer shawls and blankets for comfort. They did my laundry and cleaned my house. They took me out for coffee and even a pedicure. They came and sat with me to cry with me, or to just be silent together. They came and walked and talked with me. Their support in the aftermath was like nothing I had ever experienced before. They were each a tremendous blessing, and they all played a significant part in our journey through grief and healing.

Once the darkness of the storm has passed, it takes the help of many to restore all that has been lost. When I didn't have the strength to keep moving forward, my friends, family, and community were there to bolster me.

My commitment to personal growth is another tool that helped me greatly. Resiliency doesn't just happen on its own, and there are skills I developed beforehand that were immensely helpful in the long, dark days immediately following Tommy's death. One particular skill I had been practicing was to take my negative thoughts captive and intentionally replace those lies with the truth. This was crucial for keeping me grounded, especially in those early days. My mind was a battlefield. Every day I had to fight for my mental health as if my life depended on it, because it did. I was bombarded continually with thoughts like, why would a young man who had so much to live for do what he did? What if I had stayed home that night? If only I was a better mother, then this wouldn't have happened. I should have seen the red flags... When these thoughts began to overtake me, I would remind myself of the truth: that the answers to them would not change anything. Instead of getting lost in what-ifs and should-haves, I need to shift my perspective so I can see the light in the darkness.

Another tool that helped me is finding purpose in my pain. Helping other people who have experienced similar circumstances has brought goodness out of a very dark situation. While I cannot find the words to fully explain what I mean, it seems to follow the biblical principle of reaping what you sow. When I take actions that help sow healing in others, I receive inexplicable healing at deeper levels. This brings me a sense of hope, satisfaction, and significance that would not exist otherwise.

And of course, my faith has been an incredibly important tool. If you are going to build something great, the foundation that you build upon plays a huge role in the stability of the structure. For me, my faith has been the foundation I have built my life upon, and it gives me the support and strength to withstand even the fiercest storms.

But probably the most unexpected and powerful thing that helped me to navigate those early days were the questions I had wrestled with from my book study in the weeks preceding my son's death. Those worst-case scenarios I imagined about my marriage had nothing to do with losing my son…and yet they did. Working through them and deciding how I would walk forward if they occurred helped me cling to life; helped me embrace my faith, my growth, and my family and friends; and helped me find purpose in my pain.

Remember, I had already wrestled with the possibility of losing my husband and had decided that if that happened, it would not be a deal breaker for my relationship with God. My friends and I had also asked ourselves the difficult question, "is there any circumstance that would be a deal breaker?" While I never imagined losing my son to suicide, I had already decided that *no circumstance* would make me walk away from my faith. That question was already settled for me. And since I had already determined in my mind and in my heart that nothing would make me walk away from my faith, I didn't have to wrestle with that foundational piece of my life during a time when I could barely breathe, let alone think or process. This was crucial for me, and it allowed me to begin healing upon the sturdy rock of my faith.

Not one of us knows what tomorrow will bring. Both storms of nature and storms of life can appear suddenly, bringing complete destruction and great devastation. The good news is that no storm lasts forever. As we walk forward and sort through the debris left behind, there is hope that we can heal, and even grow. It may sound strange, but it has been in my darkest places of brokenness that I have seen the brightest light—my vision has been made clearer to more intently focus on the truly important things in life. And the next time I face an unexpected circumstance that threatens to send me over the edge of the mountain, I have powerful tools in my toolbelt to keep my feet planted on the ground.

About Kelly Mariah

Kelly Mariah is a certified coach, speaker, and trainer with the Maxwell Leadership Team. She is a certified personality and behavioural styles consultant in both the Maxwell DISC Method and iEnneagram Motions of the Soul as well as a certified Mental Health Coach with the American Association of Christian Counselors.

Kelly believes that intentional personal growth, a positive support system, and finding purpose in your pain are vital keys to success when facing adversity. She credits these three keys and her faith as the foundation for surviving and thriving in the aftermath of the tragic losses of her son to suicide and her husband to cancer.

Through her work, Kelly uses her training in leadership, behavioural styles, and personality types to help others discover self-awareness. She believes that growing in self-awareness helps us build better relationships, which in turn creates healthier home and work environments positioned for success.

In her free time, Kelly loves to laugh, dance, climb mountains, and enjoy life with her family and friends.

www.kellymariah.com
Facebook: @kellymariah2

3

Never Give Up

By Jennifer McFarland

*"Between stimulus and response
there is a space. In that space is our power to
choose our response. In our response lies our
growth and our freedom."*

— Viktor Frankl

Never Give Up

By Jennifer McFarland

"Mom, what's wrong?"

My daughter caught me in the kitchen, rummaging in the fridge for a refill of Coke. Maybe it was the look on my face that tipped her off, or maybe the fact that I had been hiding in my room all day.

This wasn't the first time she had asked me this question.

It also wasn't the first time I lied when I answered her.

"I'm just tired, sweetie. It's okay."

She turned away, shaking her head. She was only eleven, but I wasn't fooling either one of us.

There wasn't a time in my life when I wasn't full of anxiety. As a child I worried about everything—quietly, privately, so I didn't bother anyone. I wondered if there would be enough money to pay the bills. I questioned if my dad would be okay when my brother and

I were with our mom and vice versa. Being three and a half years older, I took care of my younger brother as much as I could. I worried about him, school, my friends, and my grandparents. Every day was filled with stress about something or someone.

This carried on throughout my teen years, but I thought I was happy enough. I didn't understand that other people weren't living with anxiety all day, every day.

At sixteen, general happiness suddenly wasn't an option anymore. Repressed memories of abuse that happened while I was in daycare resurfaced. This began long, lonely bouts of depression. The remembered trauma overwhelmed my mind, holding me captive for weeks and then months.

The unresolved childhood trauma seeped into my decisions, setting me up for bad decision after bad decision. I married at just barely nineteen and was pregnant within six months. Sadly, what I thought would be the start of much-wanted motherhood wasn't to be. At ten weeks, I started to have a miscarriage. No amount of prayer or bed rest made a difference. I had no idea how common miscarriages are, so I was completely unprepared for this to even be a reality for me.

At my follow up appointment, I was told I would feel weak and fatigued for another week or so, and then I should be fine. The doctor told me I couldn't get pregnant for the next three to four months.

He meant *shouldn't* get pregnant.

One month after the loss, we were evicted from our apartment. Grieving and ashamed, I reached out to my parents for help and we rented an apartment in the basement of my former home. It was winter, so my husband was laid off from his weather-dependent job. I got a job at a daycare, but I couldn't get a handle on my emotions. After two days, I couldn't force myself to go back.

One month after moving, I felt off. Turns out I could get pregnant again right away. I went to a local free clinic for a blood test and checkup, and they offered me a quick ultrasound, even though I was only eight weeks along. One fluttery heartbeat showed up, with the baby due at the end of July.

The next few months were filled with more challenges. I slipped on the ice, falling and breaking my ankle at four months pregnant. The break required surgery to stabilize the bone. Then, about three weeks before my due date, I developed preeclampsia, which made for a complicated and dangerous birth. My son was greatly affected by the medicines given to me; he was whisked away to the NICU, where he spent his first week recovering.

Fortunately, he was healthy overall. He soon came home, and we began our lives as a family of three.

Every day was spent caring for my baby and keeping up with household chores. We had hardly any money, so budgeting for diapers alone was daunting. My husband worked twelve-hour days, so I was alone with my son six days a week. The only time I had a short break was on Sunday when we went to church. This time with my son was all I ever hoped for, but the chores were a struggle and there were many lonely days.

After a couple of years, my parents offered us the unused funds they had saved for my college so we could make a down payment for a house. We gratefully accepted and found a little ranch out in the middle of nowhere. My husband was working more regularly, so we took the leap into home ownership.

Not quite a year later, my husband was badly hurt on the job. He had a head injury that required plastic surgery and caused him to have panic attacks for the next year. As I cared for him and comforted him through his recovery, I found out I was once again expecting.

This pregnancy was much more standard until the emergency c-section after sixteen hours of labour. Regardless, I was overjoyed that another healthy boy had joined our family. The boys shared a room, and they were great together.

It wasn't until a year and half passed that bigger problems became evident to me. Upon finding out I was pregnant again, my husband didn't speak to me for three days; it wasn't until we found out the new baby was the girl he wanted that he became enthusiastic. By this time, I was handling the household, raising the boys, and helping him run his new business. Although I had no office skills or experience, I did the best I could.

This was another difficult pregnancy, and I was put on bed rest during the last month. I did what I could from the couch, lying down as much as I could with one son in kindergarten and one toddler. I ended up needing another emergency c-section, but I didn't care as long as the baby was healthy. And she was, until the day after we came home. I noticed she was lethargic and looking yellow. It took a couple trips to the hospital for blood work to find out she was jaundiced. I was relying on others to get back and forth since I was banned from driving post- surgery.

For the last trip, my parents took me and helped with the boys, but they couldn't stay until the end. I called my husband to come home and help me, but he refused. I will never forget how ashamed I felt when I had to tell my parents he wasn't coming for me or our sick newborn.

Now, at twenty-six years old with three kids, I was coming to a terrible realization. My relationship was not a healthy one; in fact, it was downright abusive. Yet divorce was absolutely unthinkable to me. I wanted to spare my kids the back and forth I had grown up in, being torn between two homes and opposing perspectives. Deep in my unconscious mind, there was also a fear of them being hurt if they weren't in my care. I promised myself that I would keep my kids safe in a two-parent home, no matter what.

Since leaving wasn't an option, I tried to figure out how to make the best of a bad situation and work things out with my husband. This wasn't easy. We lived far out in the rural countryside, isolated from family and friends, which meant I was completely dependent on him for any kind of support. And any time I brought up a concern or hurt feelings, it just made things worse. My husband put a lot of effort into convincing me any problems we had were my fault. He used constant and deliberate manipulation, gaslighting, and neglect to keep me in line. The only type of abuse I didn't experience was physical, and because he wasn't hitting me, I naively thought things weren't that bad.

I worked on my many "flaws," thinking that if I fixed myself, he might finally be happy. Perhaps then I would be worthy of care and consideration. I tried my best to handle raising three young children, keeping up the housework, and helping with his business. It was never good enough. I was struggling, alone and lonely every day.

It got so bad that I began considering self-harm. I was so focused on my faults that I couldn't find one worthwhile thing about myself. I thought maybe everyone would be better off without me. I felt like my existence was a burden that no one should be forced to bear. I stayed in bed as much as I could for weeks, fighting a losing battle with depression.

One night, when the kids were in bed and I was alone, I started to plan how I could end my pain with the least amount of fallout. But as I did, I remembered my Uncle Jeff. He died by his own hand when I was a baby, and the echoes of loss and grief still rippled through my family almost thirty years later. I couldn't do that to my parents and kids. I had to hold on.

The next night, I told my husband how much I was suffering. He spent three minutes praying for me and then went to sleep. I waited for two days and nights, and he never asked me how I was doing or checked up on me in any way. I realized that if he didn't care whether

I lived or died, I would have to reach out to someone who would. It meant going against his rule not to discuss my problems with others, but I called my mom and stepdad anyway. I needed help. I couldn't do this alone.

The next couple of weeks were filled with visits to the doctor and counsellor, all financed by my family. They called me every day and helped me get a car so I could get a job. Soon, I had some of my own money for the first time in years. Even though I was bone tired from working overnight and taking care of the kids during the day, things were looking up. My husband wasn't happy with my new independence and the influences that were outside of his control, but I just put up with his complaints and ignored his requests to quit counselling. Time slipped by; months passed. We fell into a new routine and carried on.

Everything changed that December. During a mild disagreement, my husband told my two young sons to trip me as we walked through an icy parking lot. Even though I told them no, even though I tried to gently fend them off, they teamed up and managed to make me stumble. He stood by and laughed, watching me struggle as I held onto our two-year-old daughter's hand.

This event finally woke me up to the fact that I wasn't the only one being impacted by my husband's abuse. At that moment, I knew I couldn't let my children continue to grow up in an environment where they would learn and practice more cruel behaviour. In order to save them, I had to break my promise.

Even after I gathered the strength to end my toxic relationship, my troubles weren't over yet. A long, bitter custody battle kept the pain fresh and the problems constant. He would use the kids to lash out at me, then abandoned them for long periods of time when I reported his behaviour to the court.

Things got even harder when another repressed memory came

back to me. Not only had I endured all the mental, emotional, and financial abuse and neglect from my now ex-husband, but he had also sexually assaulted me. The night I had come home from the doctor, confirming the miscarriage, he wanted intimacy. I said no; that didn't matter to him.

Because of the earlier trauma I'd experienced, my brain was primed for repression to protect me. When he apologized the next morning, I didn't even understand what he was talking about. Now I was reliving that nightmare every day, with no way to wake up.

Try as I might, and I did try, I lived constantly on the edge, holding on by sheer determination. I started with the standard options, returning to therapy and medication. These things helped a little, but I couldn't afford to keep them up without health insurance. I then shifted to checking out the self-help section in the bookstore. I dedicated time to prayer and attempted to just "move on." After seeing a friend get good results, I gave eye movement desensitization and reprocessing (EMDR) therapy a try. Each of these approaches had some benefits, but I didn't get any major results that lasted long term.

I needed something to help me cope. I didn't want to drink alcohol or use illegal drugs; I never enjoyed getting tipsy and needed a clear head to take care of the kids. I was also too broke for retail therapy. So, for the most part, I relied on one not-so-healthy coping mechanism: I would suppress my emotions, keeping them stuffed down with an unending supply of sugary drinks and food. Whenever a sad, mad, or bad feeling came up, sugar would help distract me. It was also cheap, easily available, and didn't make me feel or act loopy.

I became dependent on a steady supply of sweets. Any time I tried to quit and go on a diet, I would get anxious and angry. I'd pace the floor, feeling like the walls were closing in on me. Cranky didn't begin to explain my behaviour. Rather than lash out at my family, I kept on eating.

Of course, this had a big impact on my physical health. I was dangerously overweight and constantly exhausted. My knees and feet would ache so bad at times that I couldn't sleep. My teeth were full of cavities, and some were completely breaking off. Every movement was a struggle. Basic housework was like running a marathon.

I hated how I looked and felt completely ashamed of myself for being so out of control. However, no matter how bad it was, there was nothing else that comforted me like food did.

Every aspect of my life was affected by my struggle—my parenting, my relationship, my reactions. It showed up in how I took care of myself, or rather failed to take care of myself. I felt miserable, worthless, and hopeless. The only reason I continued on was my determination not to burden my loved ones with unresolvable pain.

During the darkest times, I would spend hours reading, watching television, or scrolling on the internet. I did whatever I could to distract myself and waste the time I was awake. I hoped that by isolating myself, I could keep my sadness from contaminating my family.

Only in sleep did I find some relief. Every morning I would have to drag myself from bed, hoping against hope that nothing else bad would happen. There were brief moments of fun or joy, but the heaviness of the past abuse and present pain would always catch up with me. Always.

During my desperate search for answers, I read somewhere that the long-lasting effect from trauma was unavoidable, and the best I could hope for was finding better ways to cope or manage my reactions. Not great news. The way I was coping was ruining my well-being, slowly but surely, and I knew it was only a matter of time before I created a chronic and possibly debilitating condition. In spite of it all, I kept on looking. I decided the only way to completely fail was to give up.

And after over twenty years, the answer finally came to me.

A friend of the family had experienced remarkable relief from her emotional pain through a process called Thought Field Therapy (TFT). She invited the person she worked with, Kevin Laye, to come over from the UK to Michigan, where I lived, and give a series of talks and workshops. He would also offer a few spots for private TFT sessions.

My mom and stepdad had extra room available in their home, and the friend asked if they would be willing to host Kevin while he was in town. They agreed, and my mom signed me up for a session. I didn't know anything about the whole situation until a few days before my appointment, and even once I found out, I had no idea what would be done or how it worked. I thought at best I might learn a new coping skill; at worst, I would be vulnerable and open to a critical stranger. My pain, physical and emotional, was close to unbearable, so I was willing to take the risk. I filled out a brief questionnaire and waited for my turn.

The day of the appointment, I was extra anxious. I binged on pop and cookies to try to quiet my nerves. When I arrived, we had a brief chat while he scanned my answers. He explained that my part in this therapy was to concentrate on the memories of the painful experiences I wanted to work on, and his part was to tap on different points on my head, hand, and body. Tears slipped down my face as I thought about all the terrible times while he worked his way through the sequence of points he decided to use for me.

Within a few minutes, I felt better, calmer. Then, once he was finished, he asked me if I could feel the same emotions I did before.

I couldn't.

I searched my mind, trying to find the connection to the pain. I could remember the times I was belittled, ignored, mocked, and neglected. I could recall the gaslighting and manipulation. I could even think about the very worst traumas. Not one of those memories brought up a painful or overwhelming emotional response. They were still a part of my experience, but they didn't make me feel bad anymore.

Kevin let me know that based on how I responded, I most likely wouldn't have to deal with that same issue again. Over twenty years of suffering resolved in less than twenty minutes.

He asked me if there was anything else I'd like to work on, since there was still time left in the appointment. Dumbfounded, I said yes and explained two other major emotional obstacles. Two more sequences later, also gone.

I floated home, feeling light and bright for the first time in decades. You could even see in my face that the heavy burden from trauma had been lifted. A few weeks later, I realized I was waking up happy for the first time in my adult life.

During Kevin's visit and his talks later on, he offered to come back to train others in TFT, also known as Tapping. I jumped at the chance. When he returned in four months' time, I was sitting in the front row.

As I learned more about this therapy, I was astonished that something so powerful and effective was not better known. It was developed by Dr. Roger Callahan in the 1980s, and he published his findings in the book *Tapping the Healer Within* in 1990. He also began teaching others to use and share TFT, keeping the training process fairly exclusive. TFT is now practiced worldwide, with certified practitioners available to guide you in the techniques.

TFT works by tapping on points found in the meridian system, found in traditional Chinese medicine and used in acupuncture and acupressure. You think about the issue you want to address while tapping on specific points that correlate to the emotions you're feeling.

There's also another kind of Tapping known as the Emotional

Freedom Technique (EFT). This was developed by Gary Craig, a student of Dr. Callahan, while Nick Ortner has brought EFT to the mainstream. It has a standard set of points that are used, as opposed to TFT which takes a more custom approach. With EFT, you tap starting at the top of the head and work your way down the body while talking about the issue you want to address.

These two techniques are both helpful in different ways. EFT is great for working on a general concern with groups of people and for those who want a do-it-yourself option. TFT works well for addressing an individual's specific experience and can be customized.

It's been over ten years since I showed up to that appointment, hoping against hope that I could feel better, and I still have the same benefits from that very first session. I've been using and sharing TFT ever since. Through my work, I've been privileged to be a part of the healing journey for others. I've seen them be released from every kind of terrible trauma and grief as well as everyday stresses.

TFT has also helped me through other challenging experiences. When I was acting as a patient advocate for my father and later father-in-law, guiding them each through a cancer diagnosis and treatment, Tapping helped me stay steady for them. Tapping also helped me stay afloat in the waves of grief after they passed away. It helped me go through the long days and nights of raising teens in the midst of constant strife from my ex-husband. It's made countless other hurts and hardships bearable. During the worst times in my life, I know that I can rely on the powerful and profound benefits Tapping has brought me.

There was a time when I was in so much pain that I couldn't imagine how I would make it another day, let alone the future; now, through TFT, that pain is gone. And the only reason I found it is that I kept holding on, kept trying, kept searching for the answer. Even when I couldn't see a way forward, I never gave up.

About Jennifer McFarland

Jennifer McFarland is an author, speaker, and TFT Tapping practitioner. She is the founder of Monarch Dawn, where she combines her passion and purpose by sharing a way to heal from the past and a practical plan to create hope for the future.

Trained in TFT under the internationally acclaimed Kevin Laye over ten years ago, Jennifer shares this powerful opportunity to release lingering pain from past experiences. She has also developed Custom Made Change, helping women who discovered their ADHD later in life to connect their goals with action.

Jennifer is happiest in or around any body of water and enjoys spending time with family and her three adult children.

www.monarchdawn.com
www.custom-made-change.circle.so/home

4

Learning to Believe in Myself

By Deborah Sauro

"Your degree is just a piece of paper.
Your education is seen in your behaviour."

— Unknown

Learning to Believe in Myself

By Deborah Sauro

Growing up in the 1960s, I was always excited to follow in my older brother's footsteps and was so happy when I finally got to go to the same school as he did. I loved kindergarten, especially because I got to play with a whole class of new friends, and I loved learning. I did well enough in grades one to three. However, in my fourth year I began getting teased by the other kids. I lived in a neighbourhood that was full of mostly boys, so I learned to build forts and play games like street hockey and kick the can. As a result, I got picked on for being a bit more of a tomboy than the rest of the girls in the class. This was when my confidence first started getting chipped away, piece by piece.

Our class had a student teacher assigned to it, and during a lesson on Indigenous history he asked me if I was part Aboriginal, noting my long dark hair which I wore braided to avoid knots and my dark complexion from a summer spent outside in the sun. I told him that while I wasn't Aboriginal, I was part Japanese on my father's side. For some reason he took offense to my perceived sass and sent me to the principal's office for lying. I was devastated and ashamed about being called a liar, even though I was telling the truth. I also couldn't understand why having a Japanese background would be something to lie about. The principal called my mother to come in to discuss this, and after she confirmed my family genealogy, I was allowed back into class.

Knowing how upset I was at being accused of lying, my regular teacher, Mr. M., decided it would be best if the student teacher apologized to me. So, we were scheduled to meet during lunch hour a few days later. I went to the classroom and waited, and waited, but he never showed up. In this moment, I felt like I didn't matter—like I was unworthy.

Thankfully, this story ended well. After several minutes, I went looking for the student teacher and found him having lunch in the teacher's lounge. He had forgotten that we were to meet, and he apologized both for his oversight and for assuming I had been lying. Over time, he and I found a mutual respect. And after Mr. M. advocated for me, he became a trusted mentor throughout my education.

These experiences helped encourage me as I continued through school, but they weren't enough to combat the insecurity and feelings of shame that were building within me. While the next two years passed relatively smoothly, I continued to feel uncomfortable in myself. I felt like I was less than the other girls—less attractive, less feminine, less fashionable. I was teased by the same girls I went to birthdays and slumber parties with.

Then, in seventh grade, we were given an oral assignment for social studies. I was excited to talk about an Indigenous potlatch I had recently attended—one of the few that had been held since the ban on them, which was instituted in the late 1800s, had been lifted in the 1950s. The potlatch is a ceremonial gathering to affirm status, reaffirm family, and redistribute wealth among the community. We had been invited by a family friend who was bestowing Indigenous names and status on her daughters, and we were one of only three non-Indigenous families included in the ceremony. It had been such an honour to be included. Despite being insecure about giving an oral presentation, I was eager to share this experience with my class. However, my teacher didn't believe that I had attended a potlach because he was unaware the ban had been rescinded. Once again, my mother had to come to the school to confirm my story. Being accused of lying for a second time began an uncomfortable relationship with schooling that carried on throughout my high school years.

The social environment I was in did not help my confidence levels. The high school I attended was known for its very strong cliques. There were the jocks, the rich kids, the brainiacs, the druggies, and then there were the misfits that really didn't relate to any particular group. Being from a middle class, non-athletic family, I fit in best with the latter; I had friends with people in each of the different cliques, but I wasn't really accepted into any of them. The closest I came to fitting into a group was being a smoker. I would spend my break in the "smoke hole" with the other outsiders, where no one ever judged anyone else.

The insecurities I felt at school were amplified by the verbal and emotional abuse I received from my grandfather and uncle. Once the alcohol started flowing at family gatherings, I became a target of "teasing" that often ended with me in a bathroom in tears. I was told over and over that I was fat, stupid, and ugly—that I was never going to be as good as my older cousins, who were smart and beautiful and carried the same last name as my uncle and grandfather. I would never be enough. This, combined with the pressure to fit in at school, started to affect my health. I began to struggle with severe eczema, migraines, lack of appetite, weight loss, stuttering, and nervous shaking.

I worked hard for the first couple of years of high school, but I never really enjoyed any classes other than math and French. The teaching staff at the school was not great; in fact, several had taught my parents thirty years prior. They were uninspiring in their instruction, probably because they'd been teaching the same information for so long. I got bored easily, and in grade ten I started skipping several classes to sit in the cafeteria and read, study, play backgammon, or work on the sets for the year-end musical production.

In grade eleven I hardly went to any classes at all, though I made sure to be present for any tests and managed to get a passing grade in all my classes. One of my math teachers even went to the school board to request he be able to give me more than just a passing grade; he argued that since I rarely attended his classes, I was one of the top ten students by grades. However, the rest of my teachers did not share his feelings, and I was advised that I would not be welcome in their classes the following year.

Despite how poorly high school was going for me, and how little interest I had in being there, dropping out was never an option. Due to familial and societal expectations, I believed I needed to finish high school and get my diploma. I felt that I wouldn't be successful in the future without that piece of paper. So, I decided to change schools. I needed to be away from the environment I was in and go somewhere I could buckle down and focus. I applied to transfer and got approved by the school board to start grade twelve at a new school.

I arrived in September with a positive attitude, looking forward to a fresh start with fresh teachers. However, when I went to find my class schedule, I was told that I wasn't registered. After some research, my counsellor found out that my approved transfer had not been entered into the school's records. I spent a week sitting in the counselling offices before they finally got me registered—but when I went to get my schedule, they had registered me in grade eight. Each day I would go to the office to check on my schedule only to be told it hadn't been entered. The principal of school told me I need to attend the classes regardless of what grade they were; I refused, instead choosing to sit in the cafeteria or counselling offices and read. According to my counsellor, the principal decided at that point that I was a problem student and labelled me as such.

The school managed to register me up a grade each week, so it wound up taking nearly six weeks in total to get me entered in grade twelve classes. By then my teachers didn't believe that I hadn't been skipping, and the administrators did not help clarify the situation. Once again, I felt like I was being labeled a liar, and that I was stupid and worthless.

My counsellor felt it would be better to get me enrolled in a work experience program to cover the missing classes rather than subject me to an uncomfortable environment. So, I got placed in a local bank where my mathematical skills could be utilized. While I wasn't allowed to handle any money, I was able to shadow the cashiers and learned the all the processes. In those days, people still paid for most transactions by cheque, and I helped file the cancelled cheques once they were completed. I loved the environment, and the people I worked with did not treat me differently because I was a high school student. However, the damage to my self esteem had been done.

Throughout all this, there was an immense amount of pressure building inside me—pressure to fit in, pressure to please everyone, pressure to do the "right" thing. The delays in my schooling ramped up my insecurity and anxiety, along with all my other health issues.

I was smoking heavily and drinking to help myself cope. I felt completely useless and like I was a huge disappointment to my family; at one point, I even considered suicide.

One afternoon in the fall, much to my surprise, my mom picked me up after school and took me to a drive-in restaurant for a bite to eat. I knew something was up, and as we sat in the car waiting for our order, I anxiously waited for the hammer to drop. My first thought was that she had found out about the drinking and smoking, which I knew my family would not approve of. My heart was heavy with the thought that I had disappointed my parents yet again.

After a while, my mom told me she had received a call from my school counsellor, who wanted to meet with her. I immediately felt ashamed and embarrassed to have caused a problem. My mom continued on to say that the counsellor had informed her that several teachers had decided I was not to attend their classes any longer as I had "skipped" the first two months of school, and that the newly promoted principal was determined to get rid of all his "problem" students. The counsellor shared with my mom that she had noticed a change in my physical and mental health, and her recommendation was that my parents should remove me from school immediately.

As my mom was telling me this, she also kept telling me that I was strong, smart, beautiful, and definitely not a disappointment to either her or my dad. In addition, she told me that my grandmother had approached her with her concerns about my health, and she had also expressed that I should take some time away from school. My mom said that I had to be the one to decide whether I wanted to continue school or not, and that her and my dad would support me, whatever I chose.

Hearing this lifted a huge weight off my shoulders, and that pressure that had been building inside me started to lessen. For some time now, I'd felt like I was going through the motions for everyone else instead of doing what was right for me, and the prospect of changing my path was exciting. I decided that I would take the rest of the school year off, and if I chose to, I could return the following fall.

After quitting school, I worked with my doctor on building new coping mechanisms. Through self-hypnosis, I was able to calm my thoughts and sleep better. I started eating better and began gaining a healthy amount of weight. I stopped stuttering, and my eczema slowly started to heal.

Finding a job also helped me feel better about myself. I started off working in a second-hand boutique with my mom and fell in love with fashion and merchandising as well as working with people. I slowly started to gain confidence, and eventually I felt brave enough to step out of this safe, comfortable surrounding and get a job where I could feel more independent. I got hired at as a cashier at Fairweather, a ladies' fashion store, and worked my way up to a supervisory role.

I gained more confidence and experience as time went on, and eventually I applied for the assistant manager position. However, when I spoke to the area supervisor, I was dealt another blow. She told me that because I hadn't gotten my high school diploma, I wouldn't be considered for the position. I had been doing the job for nearly a year, but without a piece of paper, I wasn't good enough. They eventually hired a woman with a college degree in fashion management, and I was then tasked with training her from the ground up as she had never worked in a retail position before.

Thankfully, by this time I had gained enough confidence in myself to know that I was worth better. I stayed with the company for a few months more, then moved onto a job with a family-run shoe company. The wife of the company's president had worked with me at the second-hand boutique, and she had recommended her husband contact me when they were hiring. After meeting with me and learning of my experience, he took a chance and hired me to work in the cash office in the head office branch of the company. I was responsible for processing sales, packaging orders for shipping, and balancing nightly sales receipts and cash. After being in that position for only six months, they felt that I would do well processing accounts in the customer account office. After another six months, I was asked to take on the role of assistant handbag buyer. I worked with the president to choose handbag lines for seven stores as well as receiving shipments, balancing inventory, and handling customer inquiries. Several years later, I was promoted to head handbag buyer—in fact, I was the first non-family member to hold this position in the history of the company.

All of these accomplishments helped me realize that I was worth something, and that I was not stupid. I realized that not everyone felt I was worth less because I hadn't graduated high school. My co-workers and I were equals.

As I slowly started believing in my own worth, I realized that I needed to take back my strength and dignity from the people who thought they could control it. At a family dinner after my grandparents had passed, I confronted my uncle and told him he would no longer have power in my life—that I was done letting him bully me. He was stunned that I would accuse him of this, and he never apologized and never showed any remorse, but it was still a defining moment for me. It helped me believe in myself and showed me that I had the strength to handle anything.

After six years with the shoe company, I followed a dream and went back to school to become a professional makeup artist. I loved the industry, and I'm glad I gave it a shot, but it didn't work out in the end. It was nearly impossible to get into the local union, and you couldn't work in film or television without being a member. After two years of doing small jobs and volunteering for many productions, getting nowhere and going further into debt, I chose to leave the industry and took the biggest risk of my life by interviewing for a sales position on a cruise ship where I would be away from my family and friends for six months at a time. I had an honest discussion with the personnel director regarding my education, and she felt my experience was just as important, probably more so, than a high school diploma. Just eight days later, I was flying across the country to join a cruise ship.

That decision turned out better than I ever could have expected. I was hired as a sales associate in the gift shops and loved the job and the lifestyle that came with it. We worked long hours but had time off whenever we were in a port. I quickly moved up to being an assistant manager for the three onboard shops. I was responsible for scheduling on-board promotions and advertisements in the ship's daily flyer, and I was also tasked with commentating the on-board fashion shows and doing live announcements. I was terrified of doing these live events, but I also knew that I had to overcome my fear and insecurity in order to prove to myself that in fact I was smart, strong, and resilient.

I loved my job on board the ship, including the travel, the new skills I got to learn, and the amazing lifelong friends that I met. I likely would have stayed on board ships for a long time had I not met the love of my life and decided to settle back on land, beginning the best chapter of my life.

I have often wondered if I should have stayed in school and gotten that diploma. Today, though, I realize that that one piece of paper can never define me. My success throughout my career has come from my hard work, my determination to prove my worth, and finally, a belief in myself. I have also been lucky to have found people willing to take a chance on me and help me get started, and I have tried to pay this forward. Whenever I have been in a position to hire personnel, I have never judged a person on their education alone, but rather on their achievements in life, just as so many had done for me. And when roadblocks that challenge my self-worth appear, I fall back on what I know to be true: that I am capable of handling anything life throws at me.

About Deborah Sauro

Deborah Sauro worked in the retail sector for thirty-five years before retiring. She spent the majority of her career in management positions for several top retail companies, including Princess Cruises and Restoration Hardware. She is an avid reader, and during the height of covid she decided to try her hand at something new. Having spent years doubting her academic capabilities, she took a chance at writing and became an author in the best-selling collaborative book *The Gift in Your Story*.

Deborah currently lives in Squamish, BC, and divides her time between Canada and Italy, where she and her husband join their family to pick and press olives from their orchard.

5

Becoming Who I Am Here to Be

By Tami Goulet

"When you know yourself, you are empowered.
When you accept yourself, you are invincible."

—Tina Lifford

Becoming Who I Am Here to Be

By Tami Goulet

Hey you. Yeah, you. Do you ever feel like you're struggling under the weight of your to-do list? Or maybe you aren't sleeping well because you're stressed out about, well, everything? Do you find yourself snapping at your loved ones for no reason? Are your neck and shoulders sore from carrying the weight of the world? Have you ever wondered what it would be like to run away and start all over somewhere else? Then, right after that thought, the guilt comes rushing in because you know you have a fantastic life, yet you're not happy. What about asking, "What is my purpose in life? I was expecting something… more. Is this really all there is?" Then you kick yourself because you have achieved the life you've always wanted, yet you still feel like something's missing. My absolute favourite is when life feels like another chore—just one more thing to get through.

I remember feeling like that. I remember feeling stuck, like I had no choices or options. I remember feeling like I had to just keep putting one foot in front of the other because I couldn't do anything else.

I was feeling this way at a time when, from the outside, my life looked ideal. I had a fabulous husband, two amazing sons, and two wonderful bonus children—a son and a daughter. We had a beautiful home and a vast and fun social circle. Hubby was working at a job he enjoyed, and I was working in a career that was going places. Our lives were settled, and we were thriving. Yet even though I'd finally achieved everything I always thought I wanted in life, I was still so unhappy, and I couldn't figure out why. And honestly, I was at a place much more dire than being unhappy; I was numb inside. I didn't want to go to work. I didn't want to go home. I didn't want to go out and socialize. I didn't want to make any decisions about *anything*. What's for dinner? No idea. Go to bed? Not really, I knew I would just toss and turn. Go hang out with friends? Uhm, sure, but I wouldn't be very good company.

I was so lost. I felt like I was trapped inside a glass box that kept getting smaller, wrapped in chains that kept getting longer and heavier. I was screaming at the top of my lungs, but no one could hear me. Not. Even. Me.

I reluctantly made a decision that ended up being the beginning of the next stage of my life. I didn't know how to keep putting one foot in front of the other without completely losing myself in the abyss of numbness that was penetrating me. So, I decided that I needed to stop.

I chose me.

At the time, it didn't feel that way. I felt like I had failed at life, like I wasn't grateful for all that I had. I called myself a functioning depressive; I was smiling on the outside but numb on the inside.

I went off on stress leave from my corporate job, and I sought help from both a social worker and a psychologist for my diagnosed depression and anxiety. I believe in the benefits of seeking help for mental health issues, and I have had much success working with psychologists, mentors, and coaches in the past to help with other issues and traumas. Looking back, I should have caught on sooner to the fact that I was needing "more"; that what I was doing wasn't addressing the deepest root causes of my problems. But that was a lesson I wasn't ready to learn yet.

If you're wondering why I went to both, it's because these two practitioners were able to offer me different perspectives and solutions for what I was going through. A social worker provides support and coping mechanisms for day-to-day stressors, while a psychologist looks at any problematic behavioural and emotional patterns and helps create new, more functional ones. In my case, my social worker taught me that we are not our feelings; we *have* feelings. This realization was huge for me. It helped me externalize what I was feeling, almost like my feelings became someone I could speak and reason with so that I wasn't so caught up in and overwhelmed by them. In contrast, my psychologist was able to provide me with more scientific studies and reasonings behind why I was feeling or behaving a certain way. She was able to show me that I wasn't alone in what I was doing, thinking, or feeling and provided tips and tricks to help me cope. With this diversity, I was able to see my triggers, issues, and situations from a broader perspective, allowing for more significant healing to occur.

After about eight months of working with these practitioners, I began to see the benefits of their assistance, guidance, and tutelage. I was exploring creative ways of expressing myself and finding happiness in things I had let go of or pushed aside, like crafting or the simple pleasure of being outside in nature. I was getting my personal life back on track, and I began thinking it was time to head back to work, though I was still struggling with the thought of returning to the place that I felt had contributed to my overall state of being in a very negative way. Thankfully, I would continue to work with both my social worker and psychologist as I transitioned back to work, and there really were some good parts of the job that I enjoyed. Besides, I had no idea what else I wanted to do, and I didn't want to start job-hunting with an eight-month gap in my employment history.

Despite all these thoughts and feelings that were rolling around inside me, I started the whole process of heading back to work. If, as I was beginning to make these arrangements, I was sensing the glass box, the chains, and the screaming, well, that was just my mind being worried about change, right? At least, that's what I told myself at the time.

Boy, was I wrong. And it didn't take long to find out how wrong I was.

It wasn't long after this decision that a freak accident happened where I broke both ankles. The Universe decided I needed to be sat down and "talked to." It was done with the nudges, messages, and signs; it was done being gentle with me. It forced me to sit down and stop so I could finally see what it had been trying to show me for a long time now: that I had been ignoring my wants, needs, dreams, and passions. That I had been putting everyone else's thoughts, desires, expectations, and wishes ahead of my own.

The Universe had been trying to show me that I was worth more than I was giving myself. That I was worth listening to and treating well. That the world needed me to be who I was here to be.

So, I sat with myself. I really had no other choice; I was quite literally stuck in a chair with not one, but two air casts. Going through this Dark Night of the Soul was one of the hardest things I had to do, though I didn't realize I was going through it until after the fact.

For those who don't know about the Dark Night of the Soul, here is my quick definition based on my experience and various readings I have done since. It was a time that consisted of a much deeper and more introspective journey into myself than what I had been doing in the past. It was a genuine questioning of my life as I knew it. It was a deep dive into me—who I am, who I wanted to be, who I had been—and an exploration of the parts of myself I really didn't like.

The social worker and psychologist were helping me with my depression, but they weren't entirely cutting it when it came to this questioning of my life. I had always known there was more than what we could see, hear, taste, touch, and smell, and it looked like this was the time for me to get serious about exploring that. But where the heck was I supposed to start?

Luckily, Facebook was getting big at that time, and I was able to use it to find people who could help me with what I was seeking—help me realize and face what the Universe really wanted me to embody at this point in my life. It was here that I found my first mentors, and they started me on a journey that would change my life. I was also able to connect with like-minded individuals who have become my soul tribe. We are from all over the world; to this day, I have not met some of my closest friends in person.

As my mentors and I started exploring the spiritual world and my spiritual abilities as well as working through my queries about what else was out there, I felt like a whole new world had been opened for me to explore. My work with one mentor helped me recognize, open, and trust in my spiritual abilities. My work with another helped me find, acknowledge, and heal those deep, dark parts of myself that I'd hidden away out of doubt, fear, and shame. I worked with others who helped me recognize and heal the repeating patterns, beliefs, and behaviours resulting from my past traumas, from this life and from previous lifetimes. On top of all this, I read books, scoured the internet, journalled, meditated, and contemplated everything spiritual I could find.

As the weeks, and eventually months, went by, I finally felt like I was starting to see the light at the end of the tunnel. I felt that my lifelong question of what else was out there was finally being answered! And while I knew that my growth, learning, and realizations were never going to end, I thought I was further along in the process than I truly was.

The more you learn, the more you realize how little you actually know.

As I started being able to get around on my feet, my hubby and I began going out and socializing more often. During this transition, I realized that I was again struggling with who I was, what I wanted, and where I wanted to go in life. Then it hit me like a ton of bricks: I had essentially just exchanged the validation and accolades I had been getting from my corporate work for the validation and accolades I was getting from my spiritual mentors. On top of that, I had now added in a whole other dimension to my quandary: was I this spiritual individual, or was I Tami—wife, mom, daughter, friend, and more?

It had been very easy for me to be a spiritual individual while I lived within the four walls of my home, but it was very difficult for me to be that same spiritual individual out in the real world, where people had expectations of me and I of them. I had already learned so much about myself, but I realized that I had learned all those things in a bubble, without any true interaction with others. There were things I used to enjoy that I no longer took part in, and I was being drawn to things I used to avoid. This became another situation where I was unsure of what I wanted. I felt like I was once again letting everyone around me down, including myself—though at least I included myself this time around. I felt like I was being judged *and* that I was judging.

On top of all of this, my husband and children hadn't fully realized the extent to which I had healed and shifted. Once we left the bubble of our home, the gradual changes that had occurred when we were isolated were suddenly thrust into the spotlight. It was a strange time for all of us. While my family fully supported me in my journey, the shifts in my mindset and boundaries took others by surprise, creating an unsettled feeling between my husband and me.

I of course started panicking and thought that I had done all this inner work wrong, and for nothing. That I had failed again. Thankfully, because of the work I had done on myself, I quickly realized this wasn't the case. But I did discover that more inner work was needed, starting with trusting myself more and recognizing that if I wanted things to change out in the "real world," I first needed to make those changes deep inside myself. When I felt like I needed external validation, what I needed to do was to go into myself and check in with how I felt about whatever the situation was. Was I happy with it? Did it bother me? Did I agree with it? Was there something I could do differently? Did I really want to say no instead of yes?

The other realization I had was that it was okay to be *all* of me, spiritual parts included. That I wasn't only a spiritual individual *or* a mom *or* a wife; I was all these things. I was everything I wanted to be in my life, and I needed to bring all the parts of me together in a cohesive way so that I didn't feel like I was neglecting a part of me or leaving it behind. The people around me were going to need time to adjust to the "new" me—to the reveal of the person I had always been deep inside. We all needed to be patient with each other as we learned to navigate this new dynamic.

Over time, my husband and family realized that they, too, benefited from the work I was doing on myself. I was becoming more accepting, less stressed, and more open-minded to different thoughts, perspectives, and ways of doing things.

This process has not been easy; it has been a struggle and a conscious decision. It's a choice that I still make daily, especially as I continue to grow, evolve, and understand myself better. I have been hit many times with doubts and fears of being judged as either "weird" or "not weird enough." I have been worried about what my family, friends, and acquaintances would think of me. When I started my own business, I was plagued by thoughts of not being good enough, and of clients not wanting to work with someone like me. But I've come to realize the truth behind the old adage, "Those who matter won't mind, and those who mind don't matter."

As I continue on my journey, I keep learning more about myself and the world around me. I no longer get frustrated or think the worst when something bad happens as I now recognize it as another opportunity for me to learn, grow, and heal. I have found a career where I get to work with so many wonderful clients who are learning to embody their true selves and to allow healing to take place. I am no longer afraid of being weird or spiritual or out there. I am living from a place of joy, contentment, and curiosity, and I am so much more comfortable and confident with myself and the world around me.

If you've achieved the life you've always wanted but still aren't happy, it's time to start making internal changes instead of continuing to look for external solutions. It's time to end the "I'll be happy when" cycle. And unfortunately, as difficult as it is to realize this, the only common denominator in all aspects and situations of your life is *you*. You are responsible for your feelings, reactions, and thoughts—for your own happiness, health, well-being, and love. While the people and situations around you can definitely have an influence, you are the only one who can control what you think, feel, and respond to.

As you travel on your journey, it really helps to have mentors, guides, or coaches to help you along the way. We humans are really good at getting stuck in our minds, feeling overwhelmed, or drowning ourselves in self-doubt. Having that external resource can really help you get out of your own way. We are not meant to survive on our own; it's okay to ask for and receive help.

As you start to see things from a different perspective, you will want to share this experience with others and bring them along for the ride. But one of the first things you should accept is that everyone is on their own journey, and they will progress or regress at their own pace. How and what their journey looks like is their own personal choice, and some may choose to stop because the process becomes too overwhelming for them to handle.

You must also accept others for who they are—faults and all. How can you ask others to accept you as you are if you don't accept them as they are?

Another important thing to realize is that inside every trauma is a miracle waiting to be discovered. The miracle out of the trauma of my accident is that I am now able to be more wholly myself and live a life I love. Sometimes, those miracles are easy to spot; sometimes, it takes time, space, and distance to be able to see them. Look for the things you are able to understand or be or do because of this event, and if you don't see any, then give yourself more time before looking again.

Finally, remember that this journey is ongoing. As we continue our explorations into ourselves, we find deeper and deeper parts to examine, sit with, acknowledge, and heal. It's like exploring and renovating an old mansion; there are hidden passageways and old treasures just waiting to be discovered that we will only come across as we do the work. Over time it may feel like we are revisiting a part of ourselves that we thought we had already healed, and that's completely normal. Sometimes we can't see those passageways until we have a better idea what to look for.

Releasing the expectations around what should make me happy has allowed me to find true happiness. My life is not what I thought it would be, but it's exactly what it was meant to be. My journey to get here has had its ups and downs, but the result has absolutely been worth the ride.

About Tami Goulet

Tami Goulet, the *Soulful Business Alchemist* behind Speak Your Soul Magicks, blends corporate savvy with spiritual insight to empower entrepreneurs. With over twenty-five years in the corporate world and five-plus years as a solopreneur, Tami understands the juggling act entrepreneurs face—balancing roles from parent and spouse to boss and chauffeur.

Tami combines practical strategies with magical and spiritual insights to help entrepreneurs overcome overwhelm, streamline processes, and align their business and personal energies for success. She's passionate about making complex concepts simple and easy to implement, because who has time for complicated?

As a Certified Energy Healer, international speaker, and international best-selling author, Tami's expertise has been featured in *Bold Journey* magazine, showcasing her as a beacon of guidance in the entrepreneurial world.

When she's not empowering entrepreneurs, Tami enjoys the simple joys of life with her husband and fur baby in downtown Ottawa. Whether exploring local gems or enjoying quality time with loved ones, she believes in finding balance in both work and play. Ready to turn chaos into calm and dreams into reality? Tami is here to guide you every step of the way.

www.speakyoursoulmagicks.com
Email: tami@speakyoursoulmagicks.com
Facebook: @SpeakYourSoulMagicks

6

Never Too Late

By Barbara Atkins

*"You can't go back and change
the beginning, but you can start where you are
and change the ending."*

— C.S. Lewis

Never Too Late

By Barbara Atkins

"God help me" was my desperate whisper in the early hours of the morning from my dishevelled bed, having not slept a wink yet again. That was a good day, when I had a sliver of hope for a different future. Most of the time, I thought that it was too late, that I was too far gone in my addiction to be helped at all. I often felt so hopeless that I just wanted to die. My three boys—two teenagers and a pre-teen—are what kept me here. I didn't want them to grow up with the story that their mom was a drug addict who killed herself.

"How did I get here?" was the question which plagued me then, and for some time after. I had been raised by loving immigrant parents who ensured I was given every chance to benefit from the opportunities Canada had to offer. My dad had educated himself here and bettered our family lot so that my teen years were spent living in a posh neighbourhood in West Vancouver. My family's values were such that my mom never worked; she devoted herself to the care of her home, her husband, and her three daughters, of which I was the eldest. I was an excellent student, a cheerleader, a prefect, and a leader at the YWCA in our community. Our whole family faithfully attended the local Anglican Church; I was even a Sunday school teacher. I had skipped a grade in elementary school, so I went off to university at the age of seventeen, following the perfect life trajectory that my parents had planned for me—for now, at least.

Through it all, I had this nagging feeling that I did not belong. I never quite felt like I fit in at my high school; it was like I was imported from another place and time. These feelings followed me to university as well. I continued to play the part throughout my first year, right down to dating the "right" boys. This changed when I became a hostess at a new, hot restaurant. Here I found another sort of people—people who had adventures, who didn't live at home, who drank alcohol and partied with boys. For some reason I felt like I fit in better here, especially since the guys were so welcoming.

It was customary to socialize on the premises after a shift; this included drinks, all doubles of course. And once I was accepted into the group, shots of alcohol during work became the thing to do. This was the beginning of my risk-taking behaviour. I would drink and then drive home to my parents' place afterwards. Sometimes, instead of going straight home, I'd take a fellow up on an invitation to stop by his place first, innocent as I was. It is by the grace of God that I made it home safely night after night, as I usually had no recollection of what had happened during my visits or on the ensuing drive.

I was restless. I wanted to spread my wings, to move out of the family home and discover the world for myself, away from the watchful eyes of my parents. Since I was so young, my parents considered this unwise and told me that I would no longer be a member of the family if I did. So, for the next decade I struggled to finish my undergraduate degree as I made excuses not to be home. I was majoring in languages, so I used that as a reason to study abroad, changing universities multiple times and taking years off to travel. At one point I moved to the interior of British Columbia for two weeks under the guise of helping someone open a restaurant, then ended up staying for two years. Here I supplemented my drinking by using other substances to keep me upright.

Somewhere along the way, I learned that my name, Barbara, comes from the Greek word for "stranger." Whether that described who I already was or I chose to lean into it to justify my behaviour, I'm not quite sure. Either way, I felt like it was my excuse to travel and not settle down—to be distant, aloof, and uniquely me.

Eventually, I realized that my life was no longer bringing me excitement or fulfillment. I was getting bored of the party. Maybe if I got married and had kids, I thought, I would find that elusive happiness that was part of the American dream. Much to the dismay of my parents, I married the only non-white guy I knew from the restaurant business. Perhaps I was still looking for excitement, or maybe I was just pushing back against the strict and high expectations my parents had of me. Either way, we went on to have two wonderful children together.

Unfortunately, the house, kids, and husband did not fix my problems. I grew more sullen as the days passed with no happy ending in sight. My drinking habit now expanded to include daily pot use as a means to escape from the drudgery of life as a housewife.

I went back to work in the restaurant business to get myself out of the house, which now had two little boys under two competing for my attention all day long. My husband worked in the daytime while I worked evening shifts so that we wouldn't need a babysitter. My husband encouraged me to stay after work so I could socialize; little did I know that he had company at the house on the evenings I was out. This led to a whole new episode of life filled with open marriage attempts and sexual misadventures of every kind. I thought my role in life was to please my husband, so I did everything I could think of to try and make things work, yet he was growing more distant by the day. Over time I became the typical nagging housewife that no one would want to come home to, driving him further and further away until he eventually left to find solace in the arms of another. I was devastated. I lost confidence in myself and my ability to be a good judge of character, and a belief that I wasn't good enough began to pervade my subconscious.

Now that I was a single mother of an infant and a toddler, every day became about survival. Fortunately, my parents stepped in to help me out financially, and my dad became the male role model in my boys' lives for the time being.

After a demoralizing trip to the welfare office, I was able to put my two little ones into daycare so I could work. Through a friend, I procured an office job in Vancouver's downtown core where I learned computer skills. From there I held a series of positions helping small businesses go digital. I had never actually worked a full-time day job before this point, so this was a big adjustment for me and my boys.

It wasn't too long before a friend of the family started courting me, and I fell into that relationship maybe too easily. It was tough being a single mom, which made me keen to find a suitable father figure—someone to co-parent with, to help maintain the house and the garden. And this friend fit into my life seamlessly. He already knew my boys and my family, being the godfather of the youngest, and he was so good with the kids. Being more pragmatic this time around, I'm embarrassed to admit that I'm not sure I entered this marriage simply for love, especially since my romantic feelings for him grew slowly over time. But today, our love for each other is more deep and wide than I could have ever imagined possible. We share a comradery, a sensitivity, a love of beauty, an intellectual prowess, and some good old-fashioned English manners and values that sustained us through the challenges that were to come.

We agreed to get married after he had completed a residential substance abuse treatment program, and I was hopeful that joining our family would be enough to get him to put the party life behind him. He tried, but the drugs had too strong a hold on him, and on me.

After we got married, we brought a third precious son into the world. However, in spite of the blessing of new life, there was little joy in our home as the drugs had taken a firm hold. I feel a great deal of shame around this part of my story, and although much of it has been healed since then, it remains hard to write here for all the world to read, especially my three beloved sons.

My addiction got to the point where I would rarely get out of bed in the morning to get my kids ready for school without a hit of cocaine. Once they were out the door, I could only think of taking more—that's the way addiction works. It became my husband's job to feed my need, and I am ashamed to admit that I was miserable until he brought me my doses throughout the day. It was him who bought the cocaine, cooked it on the stove, and prepared a pipe for me while I simply sat there like a lifeless blob. Once the drugs entered my system, I would smile— his reward. Then I would get up and make my feeble attempt to shop, clean, and do laundry until I needed my next hit. Our careers deteriorated; I became a stay-at-home mom, and my hubby took odd jobs. We eventually burned through every penny of our RRSPs.

My world became very, very small. I somehow still managed to attend some PTA meetings—something I was proud of as I felt like it proved I was not an addict. However, my face became a much less regular feature on the soccer field sidelines, and I missed important events. I made excuses to skip family gatherings. The neighbourhood moms still graciously invited me to their events until I stopped going because I couldn't face them or carry on a civil conversation. I dreaded going to the grocery store or the gas station; I never knew who might see me and want to talk. I could barely hold a thought because my mind was going a thousand miles per minute and my mouth couldn't keep up. I couldn't look anyone in the eye. Life existed in the bedroom and the bathroom, where I had an excuse to lock the door to hide from my kids. It took about a decade for what was once occasional and fun recreational drug use to become my worst nightmare.

All of this brought me to that point of tossing and turning in bed into the wee hours of the morning, my mind alternating between wanting to end my life because I was so ashamed of who I had become and crying out to God to rescue me. I distinctly remember asking God if he could use his fairy wand and turn back the clock on my life, promising to make better choices this time.

The beginning of my turning point came when I got into a minor car accident at a major intersection while I was speeding home from a public event, desperate for my next hit. When I got home, I realized it could have been so much worse; I could have killed someone. Something had to change before I put anyone else's safety in jeopardy, especially my children's. I was writhing on my kitchen floor in anguish, awash in tears, with no idea what to do. I no longer had any friends in my life to turn to, having chased or frightened them all away. My shame kept me from opening up to my parents, who had provided me with every opportunity in life. Something made me pick up the phone, and the next thing I knew I had dialled my ex-husband. I don't remember exactly what I said, but it was enough that he then called a family member, who called another family member, and so it went. My gig was up, and by default, so was my husband's.

Concerned and loving relatives on both sides tried to figure out how to help us. Meanwhile, we could not stop, even with our world watching. It was so embarrassing to know that they knew; I could not lift my head in their presence for fear of what they would see in my eyes.

Eventually, my mother-in-law found an outpatient clinic for alcoholics and drug addicts for my husband, who was the only identified addict at the time. I had successfully painted myself as the victim, a poor housewife who was somehow forced to go along. Everyone wanted to believe it, so they did.

On the advice of the professionals at the clinic, my husband and I started attending Cocaine Anonymous meetings together. I will never forget that first meeting. When I uttered the words "my name is Barbara and I am an addict," something shifted in me. Saying this forced me to acknowledge that I too had a serious problem with drugs, not just my husband, and that I too needed treatment. Subsequently, I enrolled in the same outpatient clinic and the doctor made a treatment plan for me.

My husband and I continued attending meetings, not because we wanted to but because it was a way to keep everyone off our backs. Sometimes we drank or smoked pot before going, but go we did. Although we were not successful in getting clean and sober at this time, we did hear that recovery was possible, and we did buy the literature to study at home so we wouldn't have to go to meetings—this approach doesn't work, by the way.

One day, I was invited to speak to my husband's counsellor, who asked why I just didn't say no when offered a drug. I said I would do just that if my husband offered me drugs again. But when that day came, I did not say no as planned. That night, when the drugs were all gone, I was faced with a moment of reckoning. Amid the gut-wrenching guilt and regret over what I had done, I realized that perhaps I was actually powerless over drugs, as they say at the meetings.

Desperate to make a change, I grabbed the program literature we had purchased and carefully read steps one, two, and three for the first time. Basically, they said I couldn't stop myself, but God could stop me if I would let him. So, I got down on my knees in a position of humility and surrendered my will to the care of God as I understood him.

This was a huge moment for me. Up until now, I had not wanted to genuinely talk to God because I was so ashamed. But that evening, I sensed God speaking to me, telling me that he would clean me up. I took an old Bible off the shelf and asked God to use it to speak to me more. The passage I was drawn to was Luke 2:19: "But Mary treasured up all these things and pondered them in her heart." My own mother's heart was pounding. I didn't love myself enough at the time to stop for my own sake, but I loved my children, and I knew I had to stop for them. Then, I heard God say to me, "Rise, take up your bed, and walk." He was asking me to get off my knees, since there was no need to grovel, and follow Him instead of the men in my life, as I had been doing for years.

After much agonizing, I decided that I had to put my children first, even if it meant leaving my dear husband, my soulmate. This was a tough decision as I thought having two failed marriages and no father for my children would make me a complete loser, but it needed to be done. Now that I knew I couldn't "just say no," I needed to leave the family home because the temptation to get high with my husband was too much for me. So, I proceeded to make plans to move out with my boys.

The next day I went to work as usual, but I had made secret plans for the kids to be picked up by my sister and my ex instead of going home after school. Then, during my coffee break, I made the most difficult phone call of my life from a public phone booth, telling my beloved husband that the kids and I were not coming home.

I returned to my desk in the office, losing my nerve to follow through with my plan, and was surprised to be visited by a former pastor whom I hadn't seen in twenty-five years. I can't help but think that God planted me in a family-run Christian organization so I could have experiences like this one. Speaking to the pastor in private, I summarized my current dismal situation. He told me to invite my husband to meet me at church on Sunday, and he would have members of the congregation pray for us. I sincerely doubted that my husband would show up, but he did. And there were prayers!

That Sunday, the kids and I returned home to start life afresh, with my husband and I as clean and sober parents and partners. We began attending meetings in earnest and did everything the doctors and meeting members suggested: we got sponsors, found a home group, and did a written set of the famous Twelve Steps.

It's been over twenty-nine years since that day; I know because that's how long I've been living in recovery. It has not always been smooth sailing, but without drugs in our lives my husband and I have been able to weather every storm together. Our marriage is getting sweeter by the year, and we are now the family we always wanted to be. Our children have forgiven us and now love and respect us again. What gives my life meaning today is family.

I have also come to understand that God heard my desperate pleas and rescued me from my hellish life. He used people to point me to the road to recovery and a life worth living. He also used anonymous fellowships such as Cocaine Anonymous to teach me a new way of thinking.

One of the biggest things I learned is that I am responsible for my own happiness; that there is nothing outside of myself that can make me truly happy. I also learned that it is by giving to others that one receives the gifts of peace, contentment, and fulfillment. In the end, I found my people, made up of two tribes which sometimes overlap: my twelve-step companions and my church community.

My path to recovery also changed the trajectory of my career. During my first time doing step five, where "we admit to God, to ourselves, and to another human being the exact nature of our wrongs," the nun I was working with told me that I was to now show the compassion God had shown me to others. Following this recommendation, I got certified in counselling and was led to work in a residential treatment setting. At first I only worked with men because the organization had no such program for women in Vancouver's Downtown Eastside. When I grumbled about that, I was eventually given the job of creating a residential program for women. It took a few years and saw many iterations, but in the end God created a beautiful, longer-term sanctuary for women, including those with children, where they could safely recover and reconcile with their past. It makes me so proud to have been used by God to impact future generations. My pain has been used for good; what more can one ask for?

I once thought it was too late for me to change my ways, but now I know that isn't true. In fact, I've realized that it's never too late to take back your life. Happiness is an inside job, and now that I see what is possible, I am determined to continue creating a life I love living.

About Barbara Atkins

According to Barbara Atkins, her primary avocation has been being the mother of three handsome sons and grandma to three talented granddaughters. In her work life, she has an undergraduate degree and counselling certification along with significant accounting and management experience. As a partner and founder of Strategic Systems Inc., she was instrumental in taking companies public on the Vancouver Stock Exchange. She then employed her creativity and ingenuity to transition small businesses from manual systems into the digital world.

Barbara is known for her passionate approach to life and for her natural leadership abilities. She turned her hard-fought experience as a single mother into her legacy when she envisioned, researched, and planned an innovative long-term alcohol and recovery program for women and their families. The result is a seven-story home offering stabilization, recovery programming, job training, childcare, and housing for up to five years at no cost to the women.

Barbara is now retired from a substantive career in Vancouver's infamous Downtown Eastside, where her work has had a significant and lasting impact. She now enjoys outdoor activities such as walking, snowshoeing, cycling, and paddling, and ran her first half marathon at age sixty.

7

Beautiful Chaos

By Missy Caswell

"It is during our darkest moments that we must focus to see the light."

—Aristotle

Beautiful Chaos

By Missy Caswell

After the accident, I laid in that hospital bed for what seemed like days, tears rolling down my face, head pounding, body blackened with bruises. Excruciating pain ran rampant through every inch of my body, yet all I could think about was that split second when I realized the car wasn't stopping. That was the moment when my whole life derailed. I found myself in a downward spiral as I tried to process what was happening and come to terms with the realization that I was very likely going to spend the rest of my life battling chronic pain and crippling depression. How was I going to go home to my children and continue living my life in this state? This couldn't be happening! This isn't the life I was supposed to live.

In the years leading up to the accident, I had been slowly getting my feet under me. I was twenty-one years old when I found out I was pregnant with my first child, and I was both excited and completely terrified at the thought of becoming a parent. My mother was a very self-absorbed person who lacked empathy and often ignored my needs; her actions and words were often cruel and hurtful, leaving me feeling very neglected as a child. But after years of struggling with a challenging relationship where I never felt good enough for her, I finally got up the courage to cut her out of my life. Although I had closed the door on that part of my life, I was severely lacking in confidence and didn't think that I had the skills or abilities to be a good parent to my child.

While my husband was feeling confident about his impending fatherhood, having had a much happier upbringing, I didn't know how to be a good mom to my unborn child and didn't have any role models to turn to for guidance. I obviously couldn't talk to my mom, and none of my friends had young children of their own. I did have a good relationship with my father, but he had thrown himself into work while I was growing up, so he had been absent a lot. Doubt was quickly taking over as I navigated this new chapter of my life, but I knew one thing: I wouldn't subject my child to the trauma that I had experienced during my own childhood.

After a very difficult pregnancy, I gave birth to my eldest son and quickly discovered that I was so much better at parenting than I ever thought I would be. He thrived, and when I gave birth to my second son a few years later, I didn't have those same fears about parenting. I loved being a mother so much that I quit my full-time job and took on three part-time jobs with flexible hours so I could be at home with my children more often. Between working those jobs, taking care of my kids, and running our household, I was always on the go! I had also begun to work through some of my childhood trauma, and I felt like my confidence and self-worth were finally rising to the surface after being bogged down by feelings of self-doubt and worthlessness for so long.

One of my jobs was at a daycare, and I really loved being with all the kids. After working there a few months, I decided to take a huge risk and try to get certified as an early childhood educator. I had wanted to be a teacher when I was in high school, but I had grown up being told by my mother that I was not smart enough to go to university. So, no matter how much my teachers encouraged me to try, I just didn't have the confidence to put myself out there and risk failing my courses. When a parent is constantly telling you that you are a stupid, worthless mistake, it's hard not to believe them. But now I was starting to realize that maybe I wasn't as dense as I had been led to believe. I began taking night classes at a local college and quickly learned that I was a lot smarter than I had previously given myself credit for.

I was finally starting to feel like I had found something I was good at. I was rocking this whole being-a-mom thing, and I knew that my purpose in life was to work with children. The fact that I was taking a step toward doing something I never thought I was capable of felt amazing, and I was so proud of what I was accomplishing. My instructor even encouraged me to go back to university to become a teacher.

Little did I know that my whole life was about to be thrown off track.

March 31, 2016, was the last day I would ever be considered a normal, able-bodied woman. I had spent the day in my backyard, soaking up the sun with my boys. We were working together to do our annual spring clean up and get our vegetable and flower gardens all prepped for planting. When my husband returned home from work that evening, I ran to the hardware store to pick up a few items so we could finish our garden the next morning. And then, as I made my way back to my vehicle, I was struck in the crosswalk by a car.

It all happened so fast. I remember my body hitting the hood of the car and then being thrown through the air, landing on the hard pavement several feet away. I had never felt fear like that before, and I instantly went into shock. As I laid on the pavement, shaking and waiting for the ambulance to arrive, I knew something was very wrong. However, it wasn't until after I made it to the hospital that I began to understand just how much my life was about to change.

Over the next few weeks, I finally learned what people mean when they say, "I've hit rock bottom." My gut was telling me something wasn't right, but my doctor kept telling me that I just needed to stay active, and that I would feel better in a few weeks. Instead, I only felt worse and worse as time passed. I felt so powerless. I began experiencing severe and debilitating panic attacks, and I found it harder and harder to get out of bed. I struggled just to stand up because the pain was so intense, and I ended up needing to use a mobility aid to move around. There were days where I couldn't get into the shower, go to the washroom, dress myself, or even do a simple task like brushing my hair without assistance from my husband or my five-year-old son. It was humiliating, frustrating, and deeply depressing. I hated that I was now incapable of taking care of myself and my family, and that others had to step in to fill that role. I was only twenty-eight; I should have been a healthy, fully functioning woman.

One morning, a few weeks after the accident, I had been struggling to get myself and my kids up and dressed. I finally managed to get everyone ready and in the car so I could take the kids to daycare and school, but as I was driving, this unbelievably dreadful feeling washed over me. I felt like I needed and wanted to end my life. I felt like I was failing at everything. My mind spiraled deep into darkness as I started thinking about what a terrible mother and wife I had become, how I could barely take care of myself most days, and how much better off my family would be if they didn't have to deal with my complex, undiagnosed medical problems.

I managed to hold myself together long enough to drop my younger son at daycare, but as soon as I got back in the car I began sobbing uncontrollably. I could tell my son was scared and didn't know what was going on. I wanted to tell him I needed help, but how do you explain something like this to a five-year-old, especially when you don't really understand it yourself? So, I drove the few blocks to drop him off at school, and then I went to a walk-in clinic. When the doctor entered the room, I completely broke down. I had never felt deep, heart-wrenching sadness like I felt in that moment. After a long chat with the doctor, I left with a referral to a psychologist, a prescription for antidepressants, and a diagnosis of major depressive disorder.

I didn't want to tell anyone about this diagnosis, so I kept it a secret for a long time. It took me a few days to work up the courage to tell my husband, and I made him promise he wouldn't tell anyone else; it took me about a year to be able to share my diagnosis with our family and friends. I was ashamed and didn't want to be associated with the stigma of having a mental health disorder. It was also hard to accept that I needed help as I had grown up being taught to hide my emotions. Feelings were a sign of weakness, and I refused to be seen as a weak person—thank you, childhood trauma!

By the fall, after seeing an array of healthcare professionals every single week, I finally received a diagnosis of fibromyalgia, an auto-immune disease with no cure. I struggled to come to terms with the fact that my instinct had been right; I really was going to live with chronic pain for the rest of my life, and I would likely struggle with my mobility in the future. I very quickly became a hot mess again, and not the funny hot mess mom who forgets to bring homemade cookies to the bake sale. I was the unhinged, barely-keeping-it-together hot mess mom. I began worrying about what this diagnosis meant for my family and questioning whether I had the strength to live in pain for the remainder of my life. My children needed a mother to take care of them, and my husband hadn't signed up to be the caregiver of a disabled wife. I felt like a huge burden.

Within a year of the accident, I had seen what felt like every specialist you could possibly think of. I discovered that the injuries I sustained during the accident had brought on early-onset osteoarthritis in my hips, which explained why I was struggling to walk. I also learned I had damage to the disks in my neck and back, tendonitis in my shoulder, and—after being hospitalized with migraines that were accompanied by signs of a head injury—post-concussion syndrome. Yay me!

By this point I had dropped out of school, lost my jobs, and begun spending my days going from appointment to appointment where I was poked and prodded by an endless list of specialists and healthcare professionals. I was exhausted, and by the time I picked my kids up at the end of the day, I couldn't function. I experienced more bad days than good ones back then. I needed help, but I couldn't afford full-time daycare for our toddler, and my husband was working long shifts trying to build a business and support our family now that I didn't have an income. So, I began to rely on my mother-in-law and father-in-law to help care for my children. Although I will always be grateful for their help, I couldn't rid myself of that feeling of guilt that I couldn't be the mother I wanted to be, no matter how hard I tried. I felt like I was becoming a neglectful parent, just like my mother had been.

My body was broken, and I was now defined by my disabilities. I started to notice more and more how people would go out of their way to avoid me because, let's be honest, interacting with a disabled person makes most people uncomfortable. I became increasingly aware of the looks of pity and judgment directed toward me when parents would ask my son who their mom was and he would say "she's the one with the walking stick" or "that's my mom in the wheelchair." It was humiliating, and I began to truly believe I was inferior to the other moms around me.

As an extrovert, these experiences majorly impacted my self-worth. I became very disconnected from my family and friends, falling deeper into depression.

For years, I followed my upbringing and bottled up my emotions as I tried to navigate this new life. That all changed when I found a wonderful psychologist whom I ended up working closely with for several years. She taught me how to heal my spirit and accept my new body and its "faults," as I liked to call them back then. Even after seeing her, though, life was still very challenging. There were days—sometimes weeks—where I couldn't get out of bed because a migraine had completely debilitated me, or because the musculo-skeletal pain was so bad that I couldn't even stand up. There were too many days where I couldn't get my kids to school or daycare and I resorted to setting them up with movies and snacks, hoping that it would keep them occupied for a few hours while I lay in bed wishing my life would finally come to an end. It broke my heart to be that mom, and this experience stirred up a lot of feelings around my own childhood trauma. In the end, I was doing what I had to do to make it through the day.

Ever so slowly, things began to change. After three years of daily physical therapy, I learned how to manage my pain and navigate life in a disabled body. I also saw huge improvements in my mental health. I thought I was starting to see the light at the other end of the tunnel. Then my world was derailed yet again when my father passed away very suddenly at the age of fifty-two. I was completely devastated and entered that downward spiral into depression again, so I went back to therapy and worked on all the same things I'd dealt with the first time around.

As I worked on settling my father's estate, I had the opportunity to reflect on all that he had accomplished in his life. And as I did, I realized that at thirty-three, I might only have twenty years or so left to live. I really started to think about just how short life is and how I hadn't accomplished any of the dreams I thought I would have by now. I had thought that I would have embarked on endless adventures with my family, started my new career, and checked off many of my bucket list items. Instead, I had been living in fear of triggering pain and had begun to wander through life without purpose. I had been simply trying to get through each day for so long that I was losing sight of what was important to me. With that realization, I decided to stop letting my disabilities and pain hold me back.

My first steps toward changing my life's trajectory were finding a home that was easier for me to get around in and easing back into work in some capacity. We sold our home and moved to a neighbouring city where we could try to get a fresh start. I also connected with the teacher-librarian at my children's school, and while I was in too much pain to work with small children, she was able to find ways for me to help in whatever capacity I could. This was when my life really started to shift once again.

I became friends with that teacher and jokingly mentioned one day that her job was my dream career. In response, she encouraged me to go back to school. At first I reverted to saying I couldn't possibly do it because I wasn't smart enough. Besides, now that I had these disabilities to navigate, going back to university would be impossible. She never stopped encouraging me though—an act I will forever be grateful for—and one night I finally decided to give it a try. I applied to a local university, and a few weeks later I got my acceptance letter and embarked on a journey that I never thought I was capable of. Turns out I loved being back in school, and I ended up graduating four and a half years later with distinction, two degrees, and a job offer from my local school district. I had finally done it! I had achieved what I thought was impossible and became a teacher.

My kids were ten and fourteen when I began teaching full-time and therefore much more independent than they had been when I worked in the past, but I still found it really hard to adjust to managing my work, pain, and family all at the same time. It took a few months to find the right balance between work and home life. I eventually decided to hire a housekeeper, which reduced some of the household tasks that triggered my musculoskeletal pain and made me feel less reliant on my family to step in and pick up the slack. This act of asking for help drastically improved my mood. I quickly realized that even though some days were still harder than others, having help and a purpose in life helped me push through the pain. Our family was happier than we had been for many years, making my return to work extremely successful.

My journey of parenting with disabilities has shown me that our ableist society has a long way to go when it comes to understanding the nuanced experiences of dynamically disabled people. There are still days when my musculoskeletal pain is unbearable, requiring me to use mobility aids. The next day, however, the pain can be more manageable, and I may not require the same supports. As a result, I have been excluded and isolated many times because people think I must be making up my disability for attention. The thing about invisible illnesses is that I actually experience a variety of distressing symptoms all the time; I have just learned how to mask them so I can fit into society. And because people do not see any outward expression of these symptoms, they assume they do not exist. I hope that by sharing my story of the struggles and ableism I have experienced, I can help others to see a different perspective and recognize that we can't always assume what others are experiencing just by looking at them.

Today, I understand that my disabilities are not character flaws, and I own my new disabled identity. Embodying my disabled title has been an empowering experience that has changed the way I think about myself. I am not a person who needs to be fixed or cured. *My disability does not define who I am, it is just something that I have.* While learning to live with disabilities has been physically and emotionally trying, it has also shown me that I can persevere through anything. Navigating this challenge has brought out a strength, bravery, and resilience that I didn't see in myself before.

Out of all that beautiful chaos, I have emerged as the strongest version of me. I am confidant and resilient, and I can do anything I put my mind to.

About Missy Caswell

Missy Caswell is a teacher in British Columbia's Fraser Valley area. She has a bachelor of arts and a bachelor of education degree with specializations in history, geography, and Indigenous education, as well as a certificate in teacher-librarianship. She has always been passionate about learning and helping children reach their potential.

When Missy is not in the classroom, you can probably find her embarking on an adventure with her husband, two children, and dogs. Some of her personal interests include watercolour painting, belly dancing, fibre arts, gardening, watching baseball, reading, and fostering small dogs with a local animal rescue.

Although Missy's life has been full of unexpected challenges, she hopes that her story will help encourage other moms who have struggled with trauma and devastating loss to feel a little less alone. She also hopes to empower them to never give up on their journey of finding happiness, incredible personal growth, and self-love.

Instagram: @mrs.caswell

8

Listen to Your Heart

By Peggy Meyer

*"Listen to your heart, listen to your
inner voice of wisdom, listen to your dreams.
You know what is right for you."*

— Cheryl Hamada

Listen to Your Heart

By Peggy Meyer

For many years, I believed that the solutions to my problems were somewhere out there, somewhere outside of me, and that I just had to find them. I invested countless hours and thousands of dollars on courses, programs, books, and classes. Some were focused on improving my personal life—my parenting, nutrition, exercise, communication, and relationships. Others claimed they would improve my businesses through marketing and social media or made too-good-to-be-true promises of earning money fast. Sometimes, fate would seem to intervene in the form of an ad or post promising to help me lose twenty pounds in the next month, appearing right when I was feeling bad about how I looked, and I would jump at the opportunity.

However, each time I tried to implement what I learned, something wasn't quite right. It felt off. Some parts didn't make sense and weren't right for me. Some parts didn't work for me at all. I convinced myself that I just hadn't found the right course or program or book yet, so I continued pouring more money, energy, and time into finding the "expert" that would make me successful. I kept looking for answers from people I have never met, and who had never walked in my shoes. It wasn't until I learned to look inside myself, see myself as the expert of me, and listen to my heart that I finally began to find the answers I'd been looking for.

The journey to this realization began when I was searching for a way to get out of my private mental health business. I had been a counsellor for twenty years, and honestly, I never thought I'd be one. After taking an abnormal psychology class, I realized I didn't want to work with people who were battling severe mental illnesses; I wanted to work with normal, everyday people who just needed a little help, a little nudge in the right direction. But I didn't really know what else to do, so I became a counsellor anyway. I did enjoy most of the people I worked with, but now I was ready for a change. I wanted to impact more people. I wanted to stop trading time for money, create a passive income that could reduce my working hours, and achieve the financial freedom I dreamed of. I also wanted to feel more connected to my spouse. We couldn't talk much about my work without me compromising my integrity or ethics by divulging confidential information, and that was something I was not willing to do.

At first, coaching seemed like a better fit for me as it takes clients from where they are to where they want to be. However, the more I learned about it, the more I realized coaching wasn't what I was looking for. Insurance didn't cover this service, and where I lived, it just wasn't something many people invested in. Coaching also is very similar to counselling in that it still trades time for money and impacts one person at a time. So, it was back to the drawing board.

I wanted to do something that could bring my husband and I closer—something that we had shared interests in, that we could work on together and have conversations about. After a lot of thought and soul-searching, I decided that rather than starting something new, I would take something I was already doing and improve it. I am responsible for managing the financial books for our farm, and at the time I felt like I was doing the bare minimum. I paid the bills and got all the information to the tax accountant, and that was about it. I knew I could do a better job, so I enrolled in a class to help me with QuickBooks, then another. After not getting the help or information I was looking for, I booked an appointment with a QuickBooks "expert" to get more personalized instruction. I learned a few shortcuts and useful tips, but I also learned I was already doing a lot of the right things to track and manage the money we had. This was good for our family, but it didn't fill my desire to help more people.

I also wasn't satisfied with just managing the money we had; I wanted to make sure we were getting paid for all our hard work on the farm. It was harvest season, so we were selling grain and receiving checks, but we weren't closely tracking those numbers to make sure everything lined up. I wondered, how would we know whether we were getting paid for all the grain? So, I started tracking the tickets from the elevator and matching them with the checks we received. It was not as easy as I thought it would be. I struggled to keep up with the tedious task of matching tickets to payments on top of the household and kid responsibilities. I had papers scattered all over the kitchen table, with pen marks on every sheet marking payments and what field the ticket was from so I could track the income from each field. I believed that knowing all the expenses it took to raise the crop and how much profit we made on each field would help us make better decisions. My accountant would also be happy because she would know how much income we had by state when it was time to do our taxes.

Then, fate magically brought an email into my inbox from a guy that I had used for my counselling business. Back then he had offered done-for-you marketing and webinar programs, but now he was starting a new company which took ideas and turned them into software that would make life easier for many people. This was it! Through this opportunity, I could help solve my paperwork nightmare, make sure we get paid for all our hard work, help others do the same, *and* create a passive income for our family.

I spent the next morning writing out all the things I thought would be needed to quickly solve my problem. I then sent a very detailed four-page proposal, and it was accepted! They thought it was a great idea. I started the process of turning my idea into a reality, and soon I was forming a corporation with the people from this company as partners. I dismissed the little voice that said *they don't know anything about farming* and continued to listen to my head, who was all about making an impact on a lot of people and making money for our family.

Turning my idea into a minimum viable product took longer than the three months they promised and more than the initial investment, but through perseverance and determination I now had software that saved me hours of time. No more late nights with papers scattered across the kitchen table, matching numbers to see if we have gotten paid. Now it was time to start promoting it to others. I went to shows and conferences. I talked to individuals, networked, got feedback, and brought back suggestions for improvements. I was trying so hard to make this software successful, to have others like it so much they wanted to use it, that I felt desperate at times. But my head saw this as *the* opportunity to make a lot of money to help realize my husband's dreams of owning more farmland and my dream of being financially free. So, I trudged on.

I trudged on, believing that this vision was going to work out, even when I didn't know if my marriage was going to.

I clearly remember the summer night when my husband called while I was driving one of our kids to camp. He wanted to know how much money I had invested in making this software work; I was the one who took care of our finances, and I hadn't been totally forthcoming about it. It was a moment of truth. I told him, and he was upset. He didn't know if he could trust me anymore. He told me he didn't know if he wanted me to come home.

My head kept telling me we were fine, but my heart knew we weren't. I wasn't being totally open and honest with him. I was guarding my heart. I never felt like he understood my dreams or took the time to try. My dreams and passions were harder to articulate than his. They come from a passion to help others, to make an impact, to make the world a better place. How I achieved these was not specific. His were always clear; he loves to coach sports and farm.

I trudged on, believing that this software would make my dreams come true. If only I put one hundred percent of my effort into this, then it would work. I decided to go all-in and end my counselling practice so I could focus on this opportunity. To do this, I needed help making a huge mindset shift as I transitioned from my private practice, where clients came to me by word of mouth, to marketing and selling my idea to the masses. I needed to shift my thinking from *I just threw away decades of learning from all my education, classes, courses, and programs* to extracting the skills and knowledge I gained from them to help me in this new opportunity. I also had to shift my views on selling a product from pushing people to buy something they may not need to attracting the right customers through connecting to their needs. I had to remind myself that my doubts and fears are just naturally occurring messages that serve to protect me from harm—to caution me that I am entering unknown territory. They tell me that I'm doing something new, something different. That doesn't mean I shouldn't do it.

I hired a high-performance coach and did a lot of work to get clear on what I valued, what my purpose was, and what makes me who I am. The more I got into my own personal journey and development, and the more I tried to make it fit my new focus of promoting my software idea, the more the little voice inside me whispered, *What are you doing? Something is not right. You are not being totally honest with yourself or with others. You are not in alignment.*

The more this voice whispered, the more I ignored it. My head and those helping me get this software going all said I need to do more—more shows, more networking, more social media posts—so that more people knew about it. To make that happen, I needed to invest more money, more time, and more energy. So, I did. I trudged on.

Slowly, the whispers took hold, and the first hints of change began to appear. Through my own reflection as well as the coaching process, I learned to tell the difference between what I know in my head and what I know in my heart. When my head is talking, I feel like the rest of my body is not attached—like my head is a balloon floating above, with my body nowhere to be found. When my heart is talking, there is a feeling of solidness, of being grounded, that comes from deep within my core.

During this time, through exercises given to me by my coach, I discovered my purpose: to create deep connections and memorable moments with my family, share what I learn so I can positively impact the lives of others, and have the time and financial freedom to live life fully. Once I wrote my purpose out, I could see that I was not living it. I was not getting closer to my husband. I was not making the memories I wanted. This software idea was costing me more and more—more time away from my home and kids, more tension with my spouse, more uneasiness and disconnection inside.

Still, I trudged on. After finishing a three-day show, which I spent trying to convince others they needed what I had to offer, reality set in. My idea, my software, needed a lot of work in order to be successful, and I was out of money, out of energy, and out of alignment with who I was and who I wanted to be.

I had a meeting with my partners. One suggested we needed a larger email campaign, which would cost a large sum of money each month to implement, in order to find the right customers. The other partner felt the product needed some work. So did I. I knew I couldn't continue to promote a product that didn't meet my standards. I needed to put the whole thing on pause until we knew how we wanted to move forward.

But there was one problem. I had committed to another show in a few weeks. Not only that, but I had agreed to be a panelist for a discussion about starting a successful business based on a problem I had. I couldn't be on that panel! I couldn't talk about or promote something that I didn't even know if I would continue! If I went, I would be lying. I would be a fraud. A fake.

My insides turned. My stomach was all in knots. I couldn't sleep. I didn't know what to do. I couldn't back out, but I also couldn't lie about what was going on and why I didn't want to be there.

My body couldn't take it anymore. Two days before I was supposed to go to the show, I got sick. Really sick. I spent the entire day in the bathroom expelling all the turmoil that was stirring inside me—all the internal struggles, misalignments, incongruencies, disconnection. All the ideas of what other people thought was best for me. All of it came out until there was nothing left to release, leaving me empty and weak.

I reached out to the coordinator of the show and explained that I didn't know if I would be able to make it. If this did turn out to be an illness, I didn't want to expose others to it. She agreed I should stay home. What a relief! I didn't have to lie. I didn't have to pretend my business was doing well or pretend that I was excited for the future of it. I was free, for the moment.

At this point, the real work began. I had to get honest with myself. I spent a lot of time processing, reflecting, pondering, and journalling. I went back through the wealth of knowledge from past courses, classes, books, and programs on personal development and mindset. I started integrating this knowledge inside myself instead of just passively consuming information. I worked through ideas with my coach. I started asking myself the hard questions.

> *Who am I?*
> *Who do I want to be?*
> *What kind of relationship do I want to have with my spouse and kids?*
> *How do I want to feel?*
> *What do I want to feel?*
> *What do I want?*
> *What do I want to do?*
> *What do I value the most?*
> *How do I want to live?*
> *How can I live out my purpose?*
> *Who does God want me to be?*
> *What does God want me to do?*

As I worked through this process, I started letting go of the noise inside my head—of all the information that did not fit me, that was not who I was or wanted to be. I started removing the distractions and getting quiet. And then, I started listening to that little voice inside me. I realized I knew myself better than anyone else. I was the expert of me. There were no books, no programs, or courses that would ever fit me entirely. I can learn lots of things from them, but only I know which ones I need or will work for me.

I started thinking in pictures again, something I hadn't done in decades. I envisioned that I was the conductor of my life. That I was in charge. That I had a choice. It was my responsibility and my choice to show up as who I want to be. I could be a bright radiating light, inviting and drawing people to me, or I could be a cactus standing alone, wondering why no one will give me a hug or even come near me. I can choose to listen to "experts," or I can choose to listen to my heart—my inner voice, my intuition, my gut feeling. What God wants me to do.

I learned that I have many great ideas, but I don't have to act on all of them. I now write them down, review them, and ask how they fit with my purpose. By doing this, I often find they don't fit me right now because they don't align with my purpose or the direction I am headed. And that's okay. Maybe they will fit someday, and if not, that's okay too.

I learned that in the quiet of the mind, the heart speaks. I have to take time to meditate, to pray, to disconnect from the world and go deep within to my centre, my core, my heart. Where my truth lives. Where God lives in me. I learned that I need to listen to the whispers of messages that keep coming back months or even years later. These whispers are part of God's purpose and plan for me—what I was put on this earth to do.

That day in the bathroom, when I was emptying my body of all the incongruencies, I got connected to my body, my heart, and my soul. And as I did, I rekindled a flame: a desire to speak, write, and share what I learn with others that had been flickering within me for over twenty-five years, fighting for my attention, refusing to be put out.

Through all this inner work, I realized that my contribution and impact doesn't have to be enormous or newsworthy. I can make an impact in little ways, starting with myself and my family. I can give my kids a hug. I can make a kiss last one more second. I can say a kind word. I can refrain from lashing out. I can make someone's favourite meal. I can just be still and listen.

Or I can impact others I meet along my journey. I can hold the door for a stranger, give a smile to a mom with a crying toddler, ask someone how their day is going, or give a compliment. I can also impact others by sharing what I learn on my podcast, through my blogs, through presentations and other speaking engagements, or through volunteering on boards in my community.

I'm definitely not perfect at embodying this new path. I still get sucked into clicking on those great ads or posts on social media, or into opening up that email that seems to know just the thing I need to remedy the way I'm feeling at the moment. I still struggle to voice my feelings to those close to me. I still doubt myself, my knowledge, and my ability to make an impact. But each day, I work on listening to my heart a little more, and on connecting my thoughts with my heart in order to be in alignment with my truth, my purpose, and what God wants me to do.

We can all make a positive impact in the lives of others by listening and leading with our heart, and it starts with awareness. Get quiet and listen to the little voices and whispers inside you; they will guide you to your purpose. Write it out, reflect on it, and see what parts of your life are in alignment with your purpose and what parts aren't. Then, choose activities, work, and relationships that bring out the best of who you are and who you are meant to be. This is the way to make a lasting impact on the people and world around you. And it all starts with getting quiet, being honest, and listening to your heart.

About Peggy Meyer

Peggy Meyer has a bachelor's degree in psychology and a master's in social work. She spent nearly twenty-five years focused on improving the lives of others through a holistic approach to wellness, providing both mental health counselling and wellness coaching in her private mental health practice. After closing her private practice, Peggy continues to share what she learns on her podcast, Positive Solutions 4 Life. This bi-weekly show is centred around transforming the mind and body from the inside out.

Peggy and her husband have six incredible sports-minded children. She is a master organizer of schedules as well as the financial manager for their large family farm. She is a lifelong learner who is passionate about the topics of personal growth and mindset. Most of her time is spent on the road, taking kids to practices or attending their sporting events. When she is not doing that, you can find her relaxing with a book, tending to her yard or garden, preparing home-cooked meals, or enjoying a little time by herself.

www.positivesolutions4life.com

9

The Power of Breath

By Juliana Allen

"Inhale the present moment, exhale the past."

— Unknown

The Power of Breath

By Juliana Allen

From early on, I understood what it meant to be perfect. I started dancing ballet when I was four years old and continued into my teen years. I lived in a small, blue collar, conservative farming town in the Pacific Northwest, so dance was my escape, my passion, my everything. The thing about dance, though, is that you are not only taught that you must look a certain way, but you are also told you must be perfect. Nothing is wrong. Nothing hurts. No matter what is going on in your body, you must push through with a smile on your face. Hours are spent at rehearsal, picking apart how your body looks and every movement you make. You don't feel; you push, and you smile.

My family did not have much money growing up, and dance is expensive. By the time I was twelve, I was dancing five days a week on a full-ride scholarship from the ballet company, which was the only way my family could afford the tuition. Then one day, the director of the company pulled me aside and told me he and his partner were leaving, and he did not know if the new director would allow me to continue to dance for free. And that is how ballet ended for me. This was my first experience with heartbreak. Dance was my life, and although the lessons of perfection were inarguably damaging, the identity, the physical processing, and the clear direction it gave me were huge losses I needed to grieve.

My fifteen-year battle with anorexia and bulimia started right about when I stopped dancing. There are many complex reasons why people develop an eating disorder; for me, it was an expression of my obsessive-compulsive disorder, ADHD, perfectionism, and need to feel in control of my body, feelings, and emotions. I held on so tightly to this perceived control, afraid that if I relinquished any of it, I would crumble and never be able to get up again. It was not safe to be in my body. It was not safe to be in my mind. I was terrified that if I allowed myself to feel, the feelings would swallow me up and I would die.

My eating disorder kept me safe. It kept me safe, until it didn't. That's the thing about eating disorders and other maladaptive coping skills—they work great until they don't. And oftentimes, by the time they stop working, it's too late. The damage has been done.

I spent my teen years and early twenties in and out of the hospital as well as different treatment centres. The truth is, I didn't want to get better at first. I didn't want to face how bad my eating disorder had gotten. Eventually, though, I knew if I did not give my all to recovery, I would not survive. My body was shutting down. I had the choice to recover or die, and I chose to live. That simple. That hard, but that simple. I checked myself into a residential treatment centre for the last time, knowing this was my last chance if I wanted a future. And I came out on the other side.

Recovering from an eating disorder is anything but a straight line. There have been many ups and downs, twists and turns. But at the end of every day, I have always known that going back is not an option.

Over the next decade, I learned how to live. Slowly, cautiously, I began to emerge out of my eating disordered self. I went to college, began a career as a physical therapist assistant, dated, and started running marathons. I eventually met and married a man, and we had two beautiful children and opened a clothing boutique together; I was long done with my medical field days, and I had always wanted to own my own business.

This chapter of my life looked perfect in every way. I was married to an attractive man, owned a successful clothing store, had started a nonprofit that benefited people with eating disorders, and had my babies. I had everything I was told should make me happy. Everything. Yet, there was something inside of me that was screaming. Something inside of me that felt so off. I should be happy. I have it all. What is wrong with me?

Between my eating disorder and my experiences as a dancer, the concept of listening to my body was foreign to me. I overrode the most basic signals. On an intellectual level, I understood what it meant to honour my body's needs. On a feeling level, though, I could not grasp what that meant. I had not been taught how to check in with my body. How to connect. How to ask Her what She needed or wanted.

When my first son was nine months old, my obsessive-compulsive disorder came back very loudly. Every time his sweet little hands touched the floor, my mind spun into thoughts about the germs that could be there. Every time a toy dropped and he put it in his mouth, I was convinced he would get sick and die. This was the first major sign in my body that something was off. The OCD became unmanageable without medication, and I am so thankful to have found one that stopped the looping long enough for my rational brain to kick on.

Then my second son was born in May 2020, and it was the beginning of the end of my life as I knew it. I was experiencing the very beginning of the covid pandemic with a newborn, a three-year-old, and a first responder husband. The pregnancy had been hard, the delivery was traumatic, and my body did not recover well. The stress of the world was too much. The stress in my daily life was too much. And all of this was overshadowed by this feeling inside that something was wrong. I did not have words for what was going on; I just felt off.

I remember talking with my naturopath over Zoom one day, and she looked me in the eyes and said, "You have to figure something out. Your body is screaming at you. I can't tell you what it is, but you need to figure something out." In that moment, I had to admit to myself that what I knew was happening. I knew the truth of who I was, and denying it was destroying my body. So, at thirty-five years old, married with two young children, I finally let myself breathe the words into existence.

This was not an easy step to take. I knew I had to tell my husband, but when I told him, my whole life would change. I wouldn't be able to take it back. Once he knew, he wouldn't be able to unknow. How do I tell him? It was going to break his heart. It was going to break *my* heart.

I arranged a therapy session, my head spinning with all these questions. I was terrified. Terrified to lose the life I never thought I'd be able to have. Scared to lose the stability, the safety, the known. And for what? For something I had never allowed myself to experience? I was a fraud, a fake, a phony. Where do I even start?

"Juliana, you start by telling him," my therapist said. "One conversation. Start with the first conversation. There will be many, and you won't know how the future looks until you start the conversations."

As I logged off the virtual therapy session in my cozy home office, I sat in stillness. For a moment, the what-ifs were quieted. I knew it was time. I took a breath and walked downstairs.

It was the middle of the morning, so both kids were at preschool and my husband was working in his office. I stood awkwardly outside his door.

"How was therapy?" he asked.

"Adam…"

His eyes now locked onto mine. It's as if he knew I was about to drop a weight that would take years to lift off, and life would never look the same. I looked away.

"I think I'm gay. Gay gay. Like, all the way gay. Not bi, like I thought I was."

In that moment before I was able to look up and see his reaction, I felt relief. I did it. I spoke the words. I told him what had been eating away at me for years. The panic attacks, the obsessive-compulsive disorder, the knowing that something inside was off but not being able to face the truth, was all explained by this. I didn't want to be gay, and there was still a part of me that believed it wasn't true—that by speaking the words, the feelings of sexual attraction toward women would go away. But as I stood there, raw, vulnerable, exposed, I knew it was. And finally being able to say those words aloud was such a relief.

In that moment, everything changed.

We tried everything to make our marriage work. Our kids were one and four at the time, and neither of us were prepared to lose the life we had built. I was also still full of questions toward myself, full of doubt. I had never even kissed a woman, and yet here I was blowing up my entire life for something I had not yet allowed myself to be. How did I not know I was a lesbian? How? HOW? I felt an intense anger towards myself for not knowing. I felt like a coward. Like I had been lying to myself and everyone around me for my entire life. I still couldn't believe it was true.

I told myself that admitting it was enough—that I could be happy with simply knowing my truth and stay married to a man. I could push the gay away. Everything was fine. I was happy. I had to be. The denial was strong. I was still so disconnected from my body, terrified to drop into my feelings because deep down, I knew that I wouldn't be happy until I left my marriage and gave myself permission to live authentically. No more hiding. No more carrying the shame and guilt associated with being gay. I craved to be free but could not understand how to be okay with my truth.

One morning, after a particularly rough night of intense conversation about what we were going to do, my husband knocked on my office door.

"Jules…are you okay? What is wrong with you?"

On the other side of the door, I was curled up on the floor, crying, unable to breathe. I felt like my heart was breaking. The weight on my chest was suffocating and I couldn't breathe. I didn't want this. I didn't want to be gay. I knew I needed to get out, but I was paralyzed with fear. Overwhelmed. Crushed. Hopeless. Frozen. Desperate. Done.

He opened the door. "You need to do something about this," he told me. "You can't keep living like this."

And he was right.

In my next therapy session, I told my therapist that I was feeling desperate again. I wanted the pain to stop. The all-too-familiar darkness was engulfing me, and I knew I couldn't go there. I had already been engaging in self-injury again, and I was terrified to be alone because I did not trust myself not to hurt myself further. I could see the concern in my therapist's face when I recounted the conversation with my husband. When I admitted to her that I had been cutting again, she suggested we needed to try something different.

I had never heard of somatic work, but when she explained it to me, a faint glimmer of hope lit up in my heart. She explained how trauma is stored in the body, and how it made sense that I would be struggling so much given my history of disordered eating and constantly pushing my body to an extreme. She told me somatic work can take many forms, but the common thread is learning how to connect to the body and process emotions through it. I was very confused by this concept because I had always pushed my body regardless of what it told me to do. Through ballet, through my eating disorder, through marathon running, there was no listening to it. It was push and push. If it didn't hurt, I wasn't doing a good enough job.

My therapist interrupted my spinning thoughts with a simple but oh-so-telling question. "Once you cry, you feel better, right?"

"No."

"It is not a release for you?"

I was confused. "Wait...*people feel better after they cry?*"

It was at that moment I realized how disconnected from my body I was. Not only did I have no idea what my body was feeling, I also had no idea how to process emotions—no idea how to *be* with myself. Every time I started to feel, I did anything I could to stop the feelings before they overwhelmed me. Because once they did that, I was afraid I would hurt myself. I felt powerless to the desperation, and all I knew how to do was run away from my feelings.

As I thought more about trying something somatic, fear began to rise. What will happen when I start to feel? Will I be safe? Yet I did not want to run away from myself anymore. I did not want to continue to fear being overwhelmed by my feelings. I needed to try something different. So, I booked a session with a breathwork facilitator by reaching out to someone on social media whom I felt I could relate to. That simple, yet that hard.

"What brought you to try breathwork?" the facilitator asked over my first virtual breathwork session.

"I came out as a lesbian to my husband, and I am so scared to feel because if I feel, I will become desperate. If I become desperate, I am afraid I will hurt myself again. I struggled with an eating disorder and self-injury for a long time, and I've been cutting again. I have been in therapy for twenty-five years and I don't understand how anyone feels better after they cry."

The facilitator looked at me with such gentle compassion. Then she validated my fears, walked with me through the resistance, and held space for me to feel. I was terrified. I had never allowed myself to feel, because every time I did, it was so intense. I am a highly sensitive soul, so emotions were not safe. But still, I pressed on.

I remember how challenging staying with my breath was. As soon as I started to feel, my pattern was to shut down, to stop breathing. To smile and to turn it off.

"Keep breathing."

"I can't…" I whimpered through a forced smile and tears.

I was terrified.

"Juliana, don't let it get stuck, keep breathing. Let it move."

I instinctually placed my hands on my heart and folded into myself. Tears came streaming down my face.

"I'm scared."

"I know you're scared. Where do you feel that fear in your body?"

"My heart. It's heavy and dark. I can't do this."

"Keep breathing, let it move. Breathe into your heart."

I breathed. It moved. I eventually stopped crying. I didn't understand. I breathed…I didn't run…the feelings didn't consume me…

The first time I stayed with my breath and let myself feel something without immediately shutting down was a big moment for me. It marked the end of an entire life of running, of being paralyzed by fear of feeling.

I worked with my breathwork coach every week for three months. Each week showing up scared. Each week trusting her to walk with me through this journey. Each week going a bit deeper into the trauma, the history, the here and now, the unraveling of a lifetime of being disconnected from my body. Gently beginning to answer the question of "who am I and what do I want?"

You see, my loves, healing is living authentically. When I began to heal my trauma through connecting to my body, learning how to show up for Her, and getting curious about what She wanted, my world began to change. Not in a dramatic, overnight kind of way, but in a slow, steady, gradual process. Learning how to move emotions with breath has been key in stabilizing my nervous system, and consistently working with a breathwork facilitator gave me the confidence and courage to move forward. With the practice of getting curious about who I am and what I want through the breath, the next chapter of my life unfolded, and it is more beautiful than I ever could have imagined.

Today, my life is unrecognizable from what it was a few short years ago. I am divorced, co-parenting our sweet children, and fully out as a lesbian. My ex and I closed our clothing business, and I went on to become trained in breath/somatic work. I now work with people who are learning how to connect and listen to their bodies through the breath, and through the innate wisdom of their being. I continue to practice not running from my feelings every day.

Breathwork has been a gift to me. It has increased my capacity to stay present with the uncomfortable. To have difficult conversations. To show up for myself and for my kiddos. To live my life how I desire, no longer bound by the expectations of what should make me happy. To learn what I need to live authentically. It was through healing my trauma, through the body, that I have been able to stand in my truth, and I am so thankful that I can now support others in this journey as well.

About Juliana Allen

Juliana Allen (she/her) is a queer breathwork facilitator, somatic experiencing practitioner student, and certified energy guide dedicated to guiding individuals on their journey to reclaim their authentic selves. With a focus on healing trauma through the body, Juliana combines her expertise and personal experiences to support others in learning how to reconnect with their inner knowing.

Following her passion for fostering community connections, Juliana founded the membership community Healing Authentically, designed for those who have felt disconnected from their bodies, often due to trauma or the pressures of conforming to societal expectations. In Healing Authentically, members find a supportive space to learn how to listen to their bodies through somatic and energy tools and navigate the journey of reclaiming their authentic selves.

As a mother of two, Juliana loves spending time in nature and kicking the soccer ball with her kids. She is also the author of *The Courage to Hope*, a powerful memoir detailing her fifteen-year battle with and recovery from anorexia and bulimia.

www.Juliana.earth

10

Eat All the Cake

By Robyn Tidrick

*"Don't wait for things to get easier, simpler,
better. Life will always be complicated.
Learn to be happy right now.
Otherwise you will run out of time."*

— Unknown

Eat All the Cake

By Robyn Tidrick

It was January 2021, and the emergency waiting room was packed with mask-clad patients. My husband's fever was quickly exceeding 104 degrees Fahrenheit, and he could no longer hold himself up in his wheelchair. I asked for ice a few times, but every employee was scurrying non-stop, unable to keep up with the stream of sick humans flowing through the automatic door. I finally went outside and scooped up a bagful of snow from the walkway to cool his burning body. He was unable to open his eyes and could only mumble. He began to slip toward the floor, and I was just about to lose my grip when the nurse called his name. She came close and whispered, "He's positive for covid," then spun his chair around and began to wheel him away. As I began to follow her, she blocked my shoulder with a stiff arm and said, "I'll take him from here. A doctor will call you with updates." As quick as the words were spoken, they were gone. I took a few steps backward, squared my spine into a corner, slid to the floor, and cried. A kind stranger defied the six-foot rule to put her arm around my shoulder for comfort.

This wasn't our first trip to the ER. Eric has battled multiple sclerosis (MS) for twenty-six of our thirty-five years together, and as his immune system continues to decline, trips to the hospital have increased. Fevers from simple infections, and even the flu, have threatened to take his life several times, and we have come to terms with his possible fate. However, this time felt very different. This was during the height of the pandemic, and covid had taken the life and literal breath of people we knew. The nurse's eyes were apologetic, yet somehow robotic, and for a moment I considered the toll it must have taken on her to watch so many people die. For weeks on end, CNN religiously reported the daily death count and streamed images from around the world of covid-ravaged, plastic-wrapped bodies stacked in morgues, ice rinks, and refrigeration trucks. They featured dozens of stories showing medical heroes caped with PPE holding phones on video calls so patients would not have to die alone. My mind was flooded with replays of these images as I sat in the corner, wondering if I'd ever see my husband again. We'd had to put down our beloved family dog of seventeen years just that morning, and all I could manage to whisper was, "You can't die the same day as Grace."

It was well after midnight when my oldest son, Ryan, picked me up from the hospital. It was a beautiful night, so we drove to a viewpoint overlooking the Columbia River. Neither of us had much to say, so we walked for a little bit. It was incredibly quiet—that type of quiet that only new fallen snow can bring—and for a while the fears disappeared into the peacefulness. I even caught myself smiling. I watched Ryan taking photos a few yards away, and it occurred to me that he was thirty years old; the same age I was before MS changed our lives forever.

When I was thirty, I was the happiest I had ever been. After our two wild, crazy, strong-willed boys rocked my world, we added a baby girl to our family who sent my heart spinning into space. All I had ever wanted was to be a wife and mom (with airline stewardess coming in a strong second), and now I felt like my life was pretty much complete. On our ninth wedding anniversary, a few months after I turned thirty-one, we were presented with Eric's MS diagnosis. That was the first time his disease literally put me on the floor. Our kids were seven, four, and eleven months at the time, so we were not quite a year into being outnumbered by smallish humans. The math wasn't looking good for me. I pictured myself becoming a young widow and raising our three children all alone. However, as I was slowly educated about the progression of MS, my fears of his early death were overtaken by a fear of how to live this kind of life long-term.

At one of the half-dozen doctor's appointments that dished us all sorts of reading material for the newly diagnosed, we received a pamphlet that had a chapter titled something like "When Your Partner Decides to Leave." I remember feeling sick as I looked around that particular waiting room, wondering how many of the people there had been abandoned. I was frankly disgusted by the thought that someone could speak the vows "for better or worse, in sickness and in health" and then just walk away from that promise. And yet my determination to *never* be *that* kind of person would be tested over and over in the following years.

They say caregiving isn't for sissies, and it certainly wasn't meant for lovers. Enduring the perpetual losses month after month, year after year, and even into decades will wear out the soles of your shoes, along with the sturdiest of souls. Twenty-six years in, my heart is tired and I have relinquished my judgmental thoughts. When disease invades a marriage, you're thrown into the frontlines headfirst, and I offer heartbroken sympathy to the relationships that have died on the battlefield of chronic illness. Those of us who are still beating on the chest of a marriage, hoping for a heartbeat, waiting for a life-giving breath to fill up tired lungs, are not to be mistaken for heroes. We are exhausted, beat down, laying bloody in the trenches; yet somehow, we have not given up hope. We are survivors. We are determined. And we pray to have the strength and the courage to get up and fight one more day.

A few months after his diagnosis, MS ravaged Eric's body with repeated exacerbations that left him basically bedridden. This was not the age I ever imagined having to study the intricacies of health insurance, research wheelchairs, or learn how to administer injections and manage a dozen prescriptions. Yet here I was standing at Eric's bedside with a home health care nurse, learning how to care for my ailing husband. The neurologist had decided to administer chemotherapy, a standard treatment at the time. The hope was that the chemo, which is an immunosuppressant, would slow down the rapid progression of the disease by sort of tricking Eric's immune system to stop attacking his own body. The nurse hooked him up to an IV, showed me how to change out the chemo bags on the machine, and then left. She just left me there, with my three little kids and a fridge full of chemo bags right next to the Lunchables.

The next morning, I was wrangling the boys to get them ready for school. I heard Eric call out, but I had to change Emily's diaper before attending to him. When I finally got to our bedroom, I found Eric crawling toward the bathroom, IV pole in tow, too weak to walk. Emily had just learned to walk days prior, and now my husband was crawling. I put on a brave face and dug deep for the strong-willed gene I passed on to my boys. I helped my husband to the bathroom and then back to bed as I began to panic about how to juggle being a full-time nurse and a full-time mom and also keep our family business afloat. I was determined to make it work. "I can do this," I would tell myself. "I will do this."

Multiple sclerosis is a complicated disease that presents uniquely in every victim, which makes predicting its path of destruction incredibly difficult. There are a handful of symptoms that are common within the disease itself, but figuring out how and when they will exhibit is basically impossible. Double vision has robbed Eric of his ability to drive a car. A lack of balance forced him first to a walker and then to a wheelchair. Extreme fatigue has mandated the cancellation of countless social engagements, and the lack of coordination and loss of strength preempted the involuntary abandonment of every physical activity he used to enjoy. We would spend months or years getting used to life with one symptom, only to wake up one morning with a brand-new mess that required us to find a new way to cope. More doctor visits, more meds, more trial and error, more tears.

One of the most challenging and most unexpressed symptoms of chronic illness is navigating the perpetual cycle of grief. Each new loss incites a new wave of heartbreak, sending you back for another lap. And it just doesn't end; the marathon of losses has no finish line and stretches over such a long period of time. I was not prepared for the incessant emotional pain and how it would affect our entire family.

Christmas came shortly after Eric's diagnosis, and I was bent on bringing some light and laughter back into the house. I was demented enough to think a new puppy would be a grand distraction. When the kids opened the bow-topped box and a chubby Jack Russell Terrier named Buster tumbled into their little arms, generating squeals of delight…it truly was a movie-worthy moment. The dopamine boost provided a much-needed refuel of my ambition to be the best super-mom and most extraordinary wife in this disheartening situation.

Despite my best efforts, this crusade to be everything to everyone was short-lived. Somewhere between negotiating with Ryan to finish spelling homework, indulging Nick's unending questions, and unsuccessfully potty-training the puppy, I found Emily on the kitchen floor with Buster's poop squished in her toddler fist. I lost it. I grabbed Buster and literally threw him outside; I remember thinking he was in the air for quite a bit longer than he should be, and I was grateful there was a layer of snow to cushion his landing. After disinfecting Emily and conquering the belligerent bedtime madness, I locked myself in the bathroom, climbed fully dressed into the bathtub, and ugly cried.

Soon after my bathtub breakdown, I initiated a combination of therapy and antidepressants as we continued to pursue the slippery balance of managing this tumultuous life.

Through all this, my faith has been the foundation that has kept me from descending into the proverbial rabbit hole. However, this type of long-term stress can crack the bedrock of the strongest and most fundamental believer. Back when my faith lined up with my world and it all made sense, it was easier to believe. Now, when my desperate pleas to an all-knowing God seem to be met with silence, the doubts and unanswered questions have made it arduous to "work out [my] salvation with fear and trembling." (Philippians 12:2) I am constantly struggling to cling to unravelling threads that used to seem so solidly woven together. Perhaps some would call it a crisis of faith. And when I began to verbally process my fear and confusion with some of my peer group, I was met with a lack of understanding and even condemnation instead of the empathy and encouragement I was seeking. This was a time when I desperately needed shelter from the spiritual storm I found myself in, but expressing my doubts seemed to push some people away, leaving me isolated and deeply wounded. Those wounds have since healed into scars that remind me of the journey I have travelled. I am not the same as I was, but the new me has been repaired like kintsugi pottery, with veins of gold filling the cracks and replacing the missing pieces. I don't show these scars to just anyone, but I don't go out of my way to hide them either. And as I continue to wrestle with my faith, I find absolute peace in knowing that God is bigger than my doubts, and He is able and willing to walk with me and wait for me as I work it all out.

If you find yourself in this place, you are not alone. Those of us who are severely broken are in the process of being repaired, and He Himself is the gold glue piecing us back together.

Life with Multiple Sclerosis is formidable, but the way we choose to live with it can be the distinction between despair and joy. There are definitely days when I just feel sorry for myself; it's ugly and not a place I want to camp, but it's a reality. It is so easy to let jealousy and covetous thoughts consume me with the slightest trigger. Sometimes it's a couple shopping together at Costco, or lovers walking hand in hand on the beach, or even a partner filling up the car with gas. I get angry that it can be so ridiculously difficult to find a hotel room that is wheelchair accessible or an Airbnb that doesn't have stairs. I find myself resentful and frustrated when we have to cancel highly anticipated plans at the last minute because he is too fatigued to go. There is a constant seesaw between self-pity and deep empathy for the man I love. There is so much in my life that is out of my control, and there is nothing I can do to fix it for either of us.

This fluctuation of emotion is enough to make anyone seasick, but I have come to the conclusion that if I don't want to live in a constant state of disappointment, I need to adjust my attitude. As MS delivers each new obstacle, challenge, fear, or setback, having the ability to shift my perspective can make all the difference.

Eric survived his clash with Covid and was discharged from the hospital in just five days. When we got him settled back home in his comfy recliner, I asked him what he wanted to eat. "Is there any of that chocolate cake left?" he asked. Days prior, some friends of ours had had a tiny backyard "covid" wedding, and we were sent home with a massive amount of leftover wedding cake. I commenced with a little speech about the necessity of proper nutrition when coming out of a week in the hospital, but then Eric looked straight into my eyes and said, "I survived covid. I'm still here. I want to eat the cake!" And so he did. He celebrated life by consuming literally half of an entire cake.

This decision to embrace joy in the moment marked the beginning of a new era for Eric and me. We have soaked in the reality that life is fragile, and that it must not be wasted. There are days when sensible nutrition and exercise are necessary, but even more essential is to interrupt life with indulgences. The ensuing love handles that have replaced my youthful silhouette are no matter; I am thankful I still have love to handle.

This unimaginable journey has gifted me five life lessons that, when I choose to listen to my inner therapist, allow me to experience a greater contentedness with this life.

The first lesson is that **suffering is universal**. We all have encountered circumstances that make life difficult, uncomfortable, infuriating, or painful. As easy as it is for me to be jealous when someone else's life seems better or easier than mine, it doesn't take much effort to notice situations much more challenging than my own. I now have empathy for the elderly lady alone at the gas pump, and I appreciate that I have a husband who has been by my side for over three decades, and who spoiled me by filling my gas tank for almost as long. Instead of wallowing in my adversity, I choose to use my experiences to offer a greater empathy to others who are also suffering.

The second lesson is that **worry is a waste**. After all, most of what we worry about never happens! When I worry about whether Eric will live long enough to see grandchildren, I try to remember the hours and days I spent worrying about my husband dying and leaving me alone to raise three little kids who are now as old as I was when that fear was born. Worrying doesn't do anything to take away tomorrow's troubles, but it robs you of today's strength and peace.

The third lesson I have learned is that **being thankful changes your perspective**. The discipline of gratefulness has the ability to redeem even the most awful days. In her book *One Thousand Gifts*, Ann Voskamp says, "The way to keep your heart soft in a hard world is to keep giving thanks through the hard things." There is always, *always* something to be thankful for.

The book challenges us to keep a thankfulness journal, and for me the practice has been a sweet salve to weeping wounds. I could have allowed my worry to run rampant in the waiting room of the ER. Or, I could be thankful for entry #325: medical professionals doing everything possible to mend Eric's broken body. When he was admitted and I was back home in my bed, the fear of "what's next" could have filled my imagination with anxiety-ridden storylines, including dismal plots and desperate endings. Or, I could be thankful for entry #326: my sweet puppy curled up with me in bed, instinctively knowing I needed her unconditional love. When I find myself inconsolable, I can choose to pick up my journal, read the hundreds of past entries, and be flooded with a serotonin stream better than what any pill can provide. Voskamp reminds us that "giving thanks is always worth it, because the fight for joy is always worth it."

The fourth lesson is to **resolve to be resilient** —to find within yourself a genuine desire to bend and not break. Storms will come. Mourning the dark clouds, becoming bitter from the wind, or being deeply dissatisfied with bad weather will not make the sun shine.

Ping Fu, a Chinese-American entrepreneur, asks us to consider the malleable nature of bamboo: "It is flexible, bending with the wind but never breaking, capable of adapting to any circumstance. It suggests resilience, meaning that we have the ability to bounce back even from the most difficult times."

Modern psychology has presented many ways to develop resilience, but the following nuggets have helped me grow in this area: accepting that change is part of living, avoiding seeing each crisis as an insurmountable problem, making an effort to reflect on the growth you have experienced through the challenges you have faced, fighting to maintain a hopeful outlook, and—caregiver rule number one—taking care of yourself. Cultivating the ability to bend in hurricane-force winds will create a stronger, more supple soul.

The fifth and final lesson is that **it's possible to experience joy in the midst of pain**. Once you have truly known the fear of death, even the smallest joys are occasion for celebration. The pain of watching my kids and their dad grieve the relentless losses was recently rebirthed into tears of blissful wonder as I watched the coordinated effort to maneuver Eric's "off-road" wheelchair to the Oregon Coast beach he took them to as children. I have lamented that our kids did not have a healthy dad growing up, but I have reconciled with the fact that they each have a profound understanding of what it means to fall down and have to fight for the courage and strength to get back up. They are compassionate and empathetic to strangers in need, they make time to be with us, and they are absolutely determined to help their dad experience life to the fullest. The amazing adults my children have become are a product of the pain that carved out unfathomable space for joy. As Billy Graham said, "If we did not have dark clouds in our lives, we would not know the joy of sunshine."

I have to consistently work at relearning and reapplying these lessons on a daily basis. I have not arrived at some sort of graduation from the school of hard knocks. However, I can honestly say that I am grateful for the gift of perspective that this challenging life has offered us. I hate the way we got here, but I am growing to love the new viewpoint it has given me.

The circumstances of your life are most likely very different from mine, but the one thing that we can all learn from my story is to do what you can, while you can. Don't spend your whole life filling up a bucket list waiting for someday. Get in the car and drive seven hours to see old friends. Buy the tickets to see Taylor Swift just to watch your grown daughter experience it in person. Stay up all night watching a Netflix series and sleep all day Sunday. Eat all the cake. Choose joy, even in the face of adversity, so that you can get the most out of the life you have.

About Robyn Tidrick

Robyn Tidrick received her bachelor of arts in psychology from the University of Washington and has lived most of her life in Washington state. After a decade of being a stay-at-home mom, Robyn took on the role of children's ministry director at their local church and spent an additional ten years working and volunteering for the International Network of Children's Ministry. She also assisted her husband at their family business, which successfully served the community in Pasco, Washington for fifty-five years.

The challenges Robyn has faced have given her the desire to encourage others in difficult life circumstances by sharing openly and honestly about heartache and hope. Whether it is one-on-one or public speaking in various venues, she enjoys inspiring others to find beauty in the ashes and offering empathy to those who are struggling.

Robyn's four adult kids live in three different countries, and her favorite pastime is to chase them around the globe and make as many memories as possible. Recently retired, Robyn and her husband have relocated to a quiet neighborhood on the Costa del Sol in Spain, where they are enjoying the sunshine together as they work on their bucket list.

Email: Robyn.Tidrick@writeme.com

Kelly Snider

Founder of Epic Exchanges

Kelly has been a storyteller, a dreamer and a connector of people for over twenty years. As an event producer, she crafted each event to highlight her client's individual stories and needs. Since the 1990s, Kelly's story-focused events have raised over fifteen million dollars net for North American charities.

Kelly's mission has always been to inspire others through sharing the stories that connect us all. She has utilized her events, the Power of Story Conference in 2017, the podcast Epic Exchanges, and now the Epic Exchanges book series, to help others find the gifts in their stories in order to share, inspire, and transform lives. Kelly excels in finding the things that connect people; whether it is charity, food and wine, or just good conversation, she is able to see the possibilities that are often overlooked in both business and personal interactions. Kelly's generosity in sharing her own stories has emboldened many to find the freedom and the strength to share the own stories.

The Back Story

I never really thought my story was anything special and certainly not that it could help anyone. In fact, my story made me feel like a victim: someone to be pitied, someone weak.

When I was three years old, my parents fell asleep while smoking and started a house fire that took their lives. I was rescued by a good Samaritan who was passing by driving his daughter to work in the early hours of the morning. And my sister, eighteen months old at the time, was rescued by the firefighters who arrived on scene a few minutes later.

We were fortunate. We had grandparents who took us in for several weeks before my godparents legally added us to their family. We grew up with two other siblings, four sets of grandparents, and four families' worth of aunts and uncles and cousins, and we never wanted for anything. And yet, that label of orphan or adopted always made me feel less-than in some way. I felt I had something to prove: my worth, my value, my strength.

Upon my grandfather's death, we were cleaning out his apartment and I discovered a file full of newspaper clippings and other documents surrounding the fire. I learned more about the man who rescued me and found out that he'd been a teacher in the neighbouring school district. There were photos of him and his daughter, a follow-up article about him receiving a medal of bravery, and a copy of the letter from my grandfather nominating him for this very medal.

I wanted to find this man even though I estimated him to be in his eighties by this point. I tried the school district offices. I tried asking some of the educators I knew. I got nowhere.

Then I thought perhaps I could find him through his daughter. But of course, I didn't know where she might be or if she'd married or anything else. So I posted the newspaper articles on Facebook in a group dedicated to my city. I thought that there would be someone in this group who possibly had worked with her or gone to school with her who might speak up and help me get in contact.

Unbelievably, the very first comment on that post was from a woman who said, "That's me!" Then she said, "Were you the little girl?"

But that wasn't all that happened. The post started getting more and more comments: neighbours who remembered my parents and the tragedy, a firefighter who worked the scene who then gave up the profession because it hit so close to home for him and his family, the police officer who had been in his first week on the job and had to make the notification to my grandparents that their daughter and son-in-law had just passed away, and even people who had lived in the same home before and after that event.

I started receiving emails and text messages from friends who had spent the morning in tears seeing it all unfold—and some wondering why they didn't know this part of my story before now. There were so many people coming together to share their experiences and feelings around this one moment in time; a moment that was more than thirty years in the past.

This was when I started to realize that my story wasn't about weakness and wasn't something that would bring pity, but rather it was about strength—the strength to overcome and to rise up above any form of challenge. And not only do I have a story, but everyone has a story that points to their strength.

When we start to share our stories—the good and the bad, the traumatic and the triumphant—we inspire others. We encourage them to make it through their own difficult times and to keep pursuing their dreams.

Your story is a gift. And OUR stories are the gifts we can give to others.

Are you ready to dive into your stories?

It doesn't matter what stage you're at, whether you think you have a story yet or not, or you're not sure how to share it in an inspiring way, or you don't know where to start! Connect with Kelly and Epic Exchanges to get started.

Send Kelly an email:

kelly@yourstoryyourstrength.com

or visit

www.kellysniderauthor.com

And follow us on social media:

www.facebook.com/groups/yourstoryyourstrength

@Epic Exchanges on Instagram and YouTube

Epic Exchanges - The Podcast with Kelly Snider

An Epic Exchange is any interaction where one or all people leave being inspired, encouraged, motivated or even transformed. You have a story that can do this - the key is to find it, heal it and discover the treasure in it. Then use it to inspire others! Featuring tips on discovering your own story, and welcomes fascinating guests from all walks of life and experiences.

Listen on your favourite podcast streaming platform. Because every interaction has the potential to be an Epic Exchange.

The Gift In Your Story

Dive into the deeply engaging stories of eleven amazing and resilient women as they share their heartbreak, challenges, and successes on their journeys to find deeper meaning and purpose in every situation.

If you've ever struggled with self-confidence, if you've ever had your fairy-tale romance break into pieces, if you've ever wondered if your dreams will ever come true; this book will inspire you and help you identify the gift in those deeply challenging times. You will be able to reveal your own strength and resiliency in the stories shared in these pages. You may even be able to take the first steps on your own healing journey towards sharing your own story, and, in turn, use it to inspire, encourage and even transform. Because your story matters.

Available in print and digital formats

Your Story Your Strength

Smoke rose from the home in the pre-dawn light. A kind stranger stopped his car and ran to the house, sending his daughter to wake the neighbours and call the fire department. Inside, he could hear the screams of a child.

This day began Kelly Snider's journey towards discovering the incredible power of story. Power to not only understand the events of her life, but also to see patterns, find healing, foster better relationships and to discover her strengths and even her purpose. And this same undeniable, awe-inspiring, life-changing power lies within EVERY story. Including yours.

No matter who you are or what you've been through, there's a lesson, a gift, in your story. In these pages you can find that healing, that lesson or gift, and then discover your own way to share that story with the world to encourage healing in others. Take this journey and free yourself to embrace your true self and purpose.

That is the power of your story.

Available in print, digital and audio formats

Made in the USA
Columbia, SC
15 September 2024

41843441R00089